2002
ROMANTIC
IDEAS

Other titles by
Cyndi Haynes and Dale Edwards

2002 Things to Do on a Date
2002 Ways to Find, Attract and Keep a Mate
2002 Ways to Say "I Love You"

2002 ROMANTIC IDEAS

Special Moments
You Can Share with
the One You Love

Cyndi Haynes & *Dale Edwards*

Adams Media Corporation
Holbrook, Massachusetts

Published by
Adams Media Corporation
260 Center Street, Holbrook, MA 02343

ISBN: 1-55850-819-8

Printed in Canada.

J I H G F E D C B A

Library of Congress Cataloging-in-Publication Data
Haynes, Cyndi.
2002 romantic ideas / by Cyndi Haynes and Dale Edwards. — 1st ed.
p.   cm.
ISBN 1-55850-819-8
1. Man–woman relationships—Miscellanea. 2. Marriage—Miscellanea. 3.
Love—Miscellanea. I. Edwards, Dale. II. Title.
HQ801.H373   1998
646.7'8—dc21   97–30457
CIP

This book is available at quantity discounts for bulk purchases.
For information, call 1-800-872-5627 (in Massachusetts, 781-767-8100).

Visit our home page at http://www.adamsmedia.com

1. Start with the basics:
   Send flowers   Give candy
   Invest in gold jewelry   Bring stuffed toys
   Play romantic CDs   Date each other often

2. Flirt *only* with your sweetheart. This is basic Romance 101.

3. Reenact the best date that the two of you have ever had.

4. Remember to celebrate all your anniversaries:
   First date   First kiss
   Engagement   Wedding

5. Place a romantic stamp on the envelope whenever you send greeting cards to your mate.

Life has no joy nobler than that of love.
— AUTHOR UNKNOWN

---

6. Make a toast to each other every time you drink champagne together.

7. Give your love the valuable gift of your time.

8. Send an old-fashioned telegram to your love expressing your feelings.

9. Fall in love with each other all over again.

10. Set out to overwhelm her by sending *two* dozen roses instead of the usual one dozen.

11. Learn what your mate thinks is romantic instead of always doing what you think is romantic.

12. Get up early and watch the sunrise together.

13. Frame your favorite love note from your sweetheart.

14. Get rid of all the tangible reminders of your old loves. Now the hard part: Forget all about your old loves.

15. When the two of you shop together, treat her to something she would love to have but is too practical to purchase.

16. Spend the longest night of the year together (December 21).

17. Compliment her in front of her mother, sisters, friends, and coworkers. She will love you for it!

18. Dress up for an evening at home together.

19. Give her a subscription to the beautiful magazine *Romantic Homes*.

20. When your love is too busy to go out, bring home dinner from his favorite restaurant.

21. Late at night, whisper your wildest fantasies to your partner.

22. Every time that your mate does something special for you, write a nice thank-you note.

23. Plan little surprises for each other throughout the year. Don't limit your romantic gestures just to Valentine's Day.

24. Head over to the library for books, tapes, and magazines on ways to improve your love life.

25. Learn the fine art of pillowtalk.

26. Whenever you accept an award, be sure to acknowledge the contribution that your mate has made to your achievements.

27. To help you be more romantic and creative, work on developing the right side of your brain.

28. Work harder on your love life than you do on your career.

29. Seal all your love letters with a kiss (SWAK).

30. Create a romantic jigsaw puzzle using a love letter, poem, or song written on heavy paper or cardboard.

31. Give up the silly and unhealthy notion of "the perfect mate." It puts too much pressure on the relationship. After all, we are just human.

32. Host a rooftop picnic for two.

33. Spend the weekend photographing each other all over town. Use the pictures as gifts, for your wallets or your desks at your offices, and to create a great collage.

34. Set your alarm clock for fifteen minutes earlier than usual and spend the time just snuggling. It is a great way to start the day.

35. Choose a song that has a special meaning for your relationship and make it "your song."

36. Romance really is about the little things, so why not give him a Valentine Pez dispenser? It will bring back some happy childhood memories for him.

37. Bake a rich and yummy red velvet cake for dessert.

38. Write a love song for your sweetheart (you don't have to be good—it is the thought that counts).

39. When you double-date, always go out with fun, upbeat couples.

40. Have a "money is no object" date at least every few months. Go out and be wildly extravagant. Treat your love like royalty.

41. Carry your love's picture in your wallet and proudly show it to friends and family.

42. During the Christmas season, send a bouquet of mistletoe and ask your sweetheart to use it for your lips only.

43. Right now, put this book down and call your mate just to say hello.

44. Mark your mate's calendar with your birthday and all your "anniversaries."

45. Give a video library of wonderfully romantic movies.

46. For a little touch of affection, slip a greeting card under her pillow.

47. Design a unique and personal greeting card on your computer and color printer.

48. Give your partner one gift for each of the twelve days of Christmas.

49. Plan to watch the submarine races after dinner tonight.

50. Drop by your significant other's office with a fun, quirky, little gift.

51. Stop putting romance off to the weekends. Try to be romantic seven days a week.

52. For men: Know the five gifts that women request the most:

Jewelry   Clothing
Perfume   Handbags
Lingerie

53. For women: Know the five gifts that men request the most:

Clothing   Sports equipment
Gift certificates   Tickets
Stereo equipment

Love has the patience
to endure
The fault it sees
but cannot cure.

— EDGAR A. GUEST

---

54. Dare to be different and unique from all other lovers.

55. In early February, go to your local card shop and stock up on romantic gift bags and gift wrap to use throughout the year.

56. Explore the whole wide world hand-in-hand.

57. Trim her bangs. Trim his mustache.

58. Promise her forever.

59. Give to her forever!

60. Present her with an artist's sketch of your honeymoon hotel.

61. Be a devoted, old-fashioned kind of lover.

62. Keep in mind that research proves cuddling and snuggling are as important as sex.

63. In church on Sunday, share a hymnal with your sweetheart.

64. Treat yourselves to a special meal like Chateaubriand just for two.

65. Return to your honeymoon hotel and arrange to stay in the same room.

66. Reach out to your partner in:
    Good times   Bad times
    Romantic times

67. Give her a big ego by giving two compliments instead of just one.

68. When you have to be couch potatoes and watch television, at least curl up together.

69. Spend all your leisure time together this weekend.

70. When he has to be in the hospital, send a plant for each day that he must remain there.

71. *Cherish* your love. Look up the true meaning of this word and work at loving your spouse in this wonderful manner.

72. Never use a romantic gift or gesture as a bribe. We shouldn't even have to tell you this!

73. Teach your parrot to say sweet nothings.

74. Frame your baby pictures together.

75. Always reserve the "best" table in the restaurant for your dinner dates.

76. Send a little romantic memento after a special date.

77. Touch each other often throughout the day. This will give you both more feelings of closeness and togetherness.

78. Monogamy: the *only* way to live happily ever after.

79. Always act glad to meet/greet your mate.

80. Mail great date ideas to his office. Try one new date a month.

81. Learn to love yourself so that you can truly be lovable to your mate.

82. Romantic mistakes that we don't want you to make:
    Forgetting birthdays
    Forgetting anniversaries
    Being too uptight
    Being practical in matters of the heart

83. For a change of pace, spend the night together in a feather bed.

84. Keep courting each other for the rest of your lives!

85. Hire a band and caterer for your next anniversary celebration.

86. Skip the prenuptial agreement. How unromantic can you get!

87. Buy a hundred-dollar bouquet of her favorite flowers.

88. For a touch of Hollywood-style romance, rent:
    Ghost   *The American President*
    Roman Holiday   *Father of the Bride*
    Seems Like Old Times   *The Mirror Has Two Faces*
    Gone With the Wind

89. Talk at breakfast instead of just reading the newspaper in silence.

90. Order romantic bumper stickers that express your feelings but won't embarrass your mate.

91. Place a love note inside a helium-filled balloon.

92. Make her feel like a princess by presenting her with a tiara. Costume or bridal shops will be able to help you with this one.

93. Never call your unromantic mate unromantic. Just say that he is romantically challenged.

94. For Halloween, dress up like a famous couple. Yes, even Raggedy Ann and Andy will do, and they are easy costumes to make.

95. Don't let rainy days put a damper on your passion, Dance, kiss, and walk in the rain.

Love is a gross exaggeration of the differences between one person and everybody else.
— GEORGE BERNARD SHAW

96. Share a piece of wedding cake. Make it even more romantic by feeding it to each other.

97. Put a little romance into the evening meal by cooking with heart-shaped pasta.

98. Go on another honeymoon. Repeat often!

99. Make a lunch date for his favorite restaurant for tomorrow.

100. Look for great romantic specials the week before Valentine's Day at hotels and restaurants.

101. Give him books about his hobbies and interests to show that you support his other "loves."

102. Disconnect the doorbell at your busy home for a night of uninterrupted romance.

103. Kiss her awake in the morning.

104. Monogram her linen hankies with your initials and hers.

105. Give your lover hints on what is important to you in the romance department.

106. Make the first move!

107. Swallow your pride after an argument (just this once).

108. Steal a kiss.

109. Change colognes to fit your moods and your romantic feelings.

110. Lower his heart rate by cutting back on his caffeine intake. You should be the stimulant for his heart, not his soft drink.

111. Sign your Christmas cards from the two of you.

112. Serve the first cup of morning coffee in a photo mug showing the two of you. It is a great way to start off the day.

113. Be your mate's secret Santa.

114. Break "The Rules" when you feel like it.

115. Act like newlyweds even if you have been together for fifty years!

116. Serve cheesecake with raspberries for dinner and top it off with a champagne toast.

117. At the start of each new season, give a piece of jewelry.

118. Treat yourself with self-respect and you will be sexier, happier, and more attractive to your mate.

119. Unromantic words to avoid:
Nice   Fine
OK   Pleasant
Use passionate words to be romantic!

120. Start a "dateograph" book. After every date, write a little something about the evening or your feelings about your lover.

121. Give her a family heirloom:
Grandmother's engagement ring
Great-aunt's cameo
Mother's pearls

122. Give him a family heirloom:
Grandfather's pocket watch
Father's family crest ring
Uncle's stickpin
Grandfather's cuff links

123. For women only: Refrain from male bashing.

124. Try to win your mate's love and affection all over again.

125. Get a joint his/her makeover.

126. Set up a trust fund for your love.

127. Talk about each other's definition of love.

128. Write down two good things about your mate every week for an entire year.

129. Hey man, do the sixties thing—make love, not war.

130. Learn the fine art of negotiation. This is key for a long-lasting romance.

131. Take long walks together on a regular basis.

132. Share a bottle of wine from the year in which you first met.

133. Know that the busier you are, the more you will need to schedule romantic time together.

134. Act on your romantic whims. The more you indulge your whims, the more romance will appear in your relationship.

135. Snuggle during major thunderstorms.

136. Popular pet names to consider:

Honey	Baby
Cookie	Cupcake
Munchkin	Schmoopie

137. Loan her your shirts and sweaters (especially letter sweaters).

138. Take things slowly; true intimacy develops over time.

139. Believe in miracles, especially romantic ones.

140. Tonight, switch sides of the bed that you normally sleep on and see what develops.

141. Have a fun, good-natured snowball fight.

142. Keep a ton of breath mints around your home.

143. Hide a piece of good jewelry in a homemade Popsicle treat.

144. For a touch of elegance and romance, give her an engraved sterling silver comb and brush set.

145. Memorize your mate's face before he goes off on an extended business trip.

146. Give her *more* than half of your lottery winnings.

147. Five things to tell your mate when the occasion arises:
     You were right!
     You can do it.
     Bravo, bravo!
     I'd marry you all over again.
     Good job!

A man is rich according to what he gives,
not what he has.
— HENRY WARD BEECHER

---

148. While on vacation, give each other little gifts.

149. For your soft drink-loving mate, replace the Mountain Dew with champagne.

150. Write a short love poem in the icing on a cake.

151. Place an ad in the newspaper declaring your love (OK, you might not want to use your real names).

152. Paint your bedroom a deep, rich shade of red or passion pink to liven things up.

153. Learn to like or at least tolerate your mate's family and friends.

154. Kiss hello.

155. Send a balloon bouquet instead of a get-well plant.

156. Tell your mate that he is sexy.

157. Remind yourself that you are sexy, too.

158. Get married. We did, and for what it is worth, it only improved things in the romance department.

159. Dine late.

160. Believe that great love stories do not have endings.

161. During late January and February, shop the stores for romantic gifts to give throughout the year. The stores are jam-packed with them due to Valentine's Day.

162. Bring your love flowers from your garden.

163. Send yellow roses to show that you are friends as well as lovers.

164. Save all your love letters and cards from your mate.

165. Hide a tiny box of chocolates under his pillow.

166. Ask your friends for their tried and true romantic tips.

167. Hide gift certificates from her favorite salon around the house for:
     | Hairstyling | Facial |
     | Manicure | Pedicure |

168. Create your own holiday for two. If it works for both of you, why not campaign to make it a national holiday for the rest of us romantics?

169. Sweep your mate off her feet.

170. Feed each other dinner for a little touch of romance tonight.

171. Place a lock on your bedroom door to keep the little ones out, not to keep your mate in.

172. Save a bottle of champagne for a rainy day or for making up after a big fight.

173. When you get a bonus at work, splurge on a gift for your significant other.

174. Tell your mate often that you love him.

175. Plan to spend every Valentine's Day together till the end of time.

176. Give a CD of Andrew Lloyd Webber's most romantic songs.

177. Have a spouse/significant other appreciation day.

178. Give her a fabulous foot massage after her day at the shopping mall.

179. Search your hearts to find the ideal balance between you and your love.

180. Wear silk undergarments.

181. Kiss tenderly and slowly. This may be an art form that you need to practice.

182. Nibble on his ear.

183. Give her a beautiful gold heart pendant.

184. Have a caricature picture made of the two of you by a well-known artist.

185. Only give *sincere* compliments.

186. Place heart-shaped sachets in her lingerie drawers or luggage.

187. Open your heart and soul to your lover.

188. Hum "your song" on your way to pick up your love.

189. Leave work early and arrange a clandestine meeting.

190. When you can't afford a dream getaway, rent videos of your ideal destination and enjoy a movie version of your romantic trip.

---

*The quickest way to go broke
is to start loving beyond your means.*
— AUTHOR UNKNOWN

---

191. Give each other lots of back rubs during stressful times.

192. When your mate takes your hand, squeeze his to let him know that you are glad to be holding hands with him.

193. Forgive and forget. Grudge holding is *not* a romantic gesture.

194. Always, always, keep your promises to your love.

195. Consider taking his name when you marry.

196. Stop your family and friends from meddling in your relationship.

197. Try some PDA (public display of affection) today. Show the whole world how you feel.

198. Spritz your home and car with scents that your mate loves.

199. Attend a church service together and hold hands throughout the service.

200. Be sure you like your mate as well as love your mate.

201. When your partner gives you a gift, be sure to use it right away and to use it often.

202. Place heart-shaped doilies under your breakfast muffins.

203. Set up a personal foundation in honor of your loved one. You can start with an endowment of as little as $5,000. Call the Council on Foundations at 202-467-0427.

204. Tease your partner lovingly and gently.

205. Prepare a Christmas stocking for your lover.

206. Know the keys of romance:

Love	Respect
Sense of humor	Sense of adventure
Spontaneity	Sense of fun
Wanting to please your love	

207. Refer to your wife as your bride.

208. Send a variety of greeting cards, including homemade ones.

209. Celebrate Sweetest Day in October.

210. Learn to say, "I'm sorry."

211. Surprise your love in little and in extravagant ways.

212. Place fresh flowers in the refrigerator for her to find after a boring trip to the grocery store.

213. Have a romantic motto that the two of you share and live by, such as:
    "Love makes the world go around"
    "Two's better than one"
    "All the world loves a lover"

214. Ask your mate to name his favorite movie love scene and try to re-create it.

215. Take him out for a change.

216. Spoil her silly for an entire week or month.

217. Leave a cute romantic message on his answering machine.

218. Unless she requests one, never, ever, give a cubic zirconia instead of a diamond.

219. Instead of sending fresh flowers, send a silk bouquet and make the romance last even longer.

220. On a beautiful day stroll hand-in-hand during a nature walk.

221. Instead of staying at major motel chains when you travel, try a romantic bed-and-breakfast or a small country inn for a nice change and lots of ambiance.

222. Tonight, prepare dinner together.

223. Hunt for romantic settings such as:
    Beaches   Lakes
    Gardens   Mountains

224. Exchange a tiny remembrance gift at least every month or so.

225. Place confetti in your gift bags and boxes.

226. Call your significant other and play a tape of "your song" in the background while you chat.

227. Hire a caterer to prepare a small feast for two or just to cook dinner once a month.

228. Share your dreams with each other.

229. Linger, linger, linger.

230. Save all the green M&Ms for your love.

231. Give a tape of wedding music for an anniversary present.

232. Hold hands during the next wedding ceremony you attend.

233. Great places to hide love notes:
    In the book he is reading
    In the cookie jar
    Under her pillow

> Folded in his bath towel
> In pockets
> In a box of his favorite junk food
> In storage boxes

234. Be her coach at Lamaze classes.

235. Leave your radio tuned to a classical music station.

236. Place a small bouquet of violets on her pillow.

237. Most lovers serve breakfast in bed—why not try dinner in bed?

238. Always keep a current picture of your love on your nightstand.

239. Reminisce often about your wonderful times together.

240. Save newspapers from your anniversaries. Years from now, you'll enjoy reading them together.

241. Be a little outrageous in the romance department from time to time.

242. Give meaningful gifts to your love.

243. Exercise together.

244. On a beautiful spring day, rent a bicycle built for two.

245. Talk to each other about sex.

246. Look for restaurants that have beautiful views.

247. Make a trip to the card store at least once a month. Stock up on the upcoming holiday cards and all kinds of romantic "thinking of you" cards.

248. Go on a moonlit picnic instead of the usual daytime version.

249. Have an instant new chair. Sit in his lap.

250. Write a little message with lipstick on the bathroom mirror.

251. Place romantic stickers on all the love notes, date invitations, and letters that you send.

252. Instead of sending one bouquet, why not send two or three and really express your feelings in a wonderful manner?

253. Write silly, lovey-dovey messages in her fashion magazines or in his sports magazines.

---

*Flattery—telling your lover exactly
what he thinks of himself.*
— UNKNOWN

---

254. For a little touch of yuppie romance, purchase matching Coach briefcases.

255. For men only: Put her before your:
Career/Job   Buddies
Sports   Hobbies

256. For women only: Put him before your:
Career   Children
Mother   Girlfriends
Pets

257. Place a menu from a fabulous restaurant under his windshield wiper with a note to meet you there for dinner.

258. Here is a basic romance rule of thumb: Never skimp on romance.

259. Give him a sexy wake-up call when he is out of town on business.

260. When someone gives you a gift, share it with your mate when it is appropriate to do so.

261. Give him "the look" from across a crowded room.

262. Stop stereotyping each other. You are both unique individuals.

263. Take a drive or stroll down Lover's Lane.

264. Ask your mate out for a date a year in advance, just to show that you plan on being together.

265. Inscribe any rings that you give with a romantic saying.

266. Give him a facial at home or send him to a coed spa.

267. To set a romantic mood, serve a fine wine with dinner tonight.

268. Seek to make him feel appreciated.

269. Strive to make her feel special and unique.

270. Give him a severe case of goosebumps.

271. At your next dinner party, use place cards. Instead of your lover's name, write, "World's Best Mate."

272. Play an adult version of hide-and-seek or tag.

273. Send your mate a holiday letter (you know, the kind where everyone brags about the past year). Tell your love how fabulous your love life is with him and how happy you are. Be sure to include anecdotes, highlights, and vacation stories.

274. Carry a cellular phone to keep in touch at all times.

275. *Just* kiss for a whole night.

276. For a shopaholic mate, take her shopping along Bond Street and Piccadilly in London.

277. Stop trying to manipulate your mate. Let go of the need to control. Be carefree.

278. Spend every February 29th together for the rest of your lives.

279. Give him a piece of diamond jewelry for a change. We suggest:
Ring   Tie tack
Cuff links   Stickpin
Watch

280. Share a raft or blanket at the beach on a pretty summer afternoon.

281. Talk out your problems face-to-face.

282. Secretly pay off all his speeding tickets.

283. Secretly pay off all her parking tickets.

284. This is a very important key to a great romance and it sounds simple, but you must work at doing it on a regular basis—have fun together.

285. Take over for her at home with the children and the chores.

286. Send mistletoe in June. Why kiss just at Christmas?

287. Keep in mind that unexpected gifts are usually the most treasured ones.

288. Go skinny-dipping at midnight.

289. Rent a yacht for a dream getaway.

290. Be her caddie at her golf tournament and hide little gifts in her golf bag.

291. Place his phone number in the number one spot on your speed dial and make sure he knows that he holds this little place of honor.

292. Cook dinner together using your fireplace.

293. Buy matching T-shirts and wear them when you go on a picnic.

One way for a husband to get the last word is to apologize.
— PEGGY CAROLINE

---

294. Give up thinking of romance as something for sissies and wimps.

295. Send a prayer book to your mate when you know that he is going through a rough time. Inscribe the book with a notation stating that you will always love him, no matter what happens.

296. Ask your travel agent to throw together a great last-minute vacation.

297. Have a florist, a personal shopper, and a travel agent that you can count on to keep your romance running smoothly.

298. Keep in mind that moods are contagious. Let's hope your mate catches your romance fever.

299. Wish on a falling star together.

300. Create a fabulous second childhood together where you give each other the love and nurturing that you both missed in your first childhoods.

301. Place your business card in her wallet in case she needs your work number or fax number in an emergency. Write a little note on the card telling her that you will always be there in a jam.

302. Celebrate St. Nicholas night on December 6 by giving your love a small holiday gift or decoration. Let this occasion be a great start to the Christmas season.

303. Call her once a day from the office just to say, "Hi."

304. When you mow the lawn, design a message in the grass. It helps if you can look down on the grass from a second story.

305. Share anecdotes of your day with each other and be sure to include any romantic feelings that you felt for your mate during the day.

306. Make your relationship a safe, romantic harbor in the storms of your lives.

307. Give every day a festive feeling by placing little party favors at his place setting at dinner.

308. Curl up under a beautiful Christmas quilt and watch:
   It's a Wonderful Life
   Miracle on 34th Street
   The Grinch That Stole Christmas
   Scrooge

309. Create a romantic scene or message on his screen saver.

310. Take her to see a production of Rodgers and Hammerstein's *Cinderella.*

311. Always return your lover's calls promptly to show just how much she means to you.

312. Put your animal magnetism to good use.

313. Try looking at your mate with your heart *and* your soul.

314. On a rainy day, create a travel wish list of all the places that you both want to visit together.

315. Read *2002 Ways to Find, Attract, and Keep a Mate* and concentrate on the parts about keeping your love happy.

316. Have your own special ways of letting each other know when you are "in the mood."

317. Plant a romantic and beautiful rose garden for her.

318. Give 150 percent.

319. Add a little excitement to your dates by double-dating with different kinds of people. Just remember always to go out with happy couples.

320. Start a collection of knickknacks or other kinds of memorabilia that you both would enjoy having and collecting.

321. Give your love a sterling silver letter opener to open your love letters.

322. Strive to be a happy couple, not a perfect couple.

323. Ask for hugs and kisses instead of material gifts.

324. Always keep your mate's confidences, no matter how juicy they are.

325. Five things to tell your love on a regular basis:
You are wonderful	I'll always love you
You are the best	You are amazing
You are my one true love	

326. Make the necessary sacrifices for your relationship.

327. On a regular basis, get away together from:
Your job	Your children
The real world	

328. Throughout the year, shop for little gifts for your mate to help ensure that you will have lots of "perfect" gifts instead of last-minute leftovers.

329. When it comes to romance, keep in mind that it is better to err on the side of too much instead of too little.

330. Ask, not demand, that your lover make romantic gestures that are important to you.

331. Have a band play "your song" at the next wedding or dance that you attend together.

332. When you are wanting to be romantic, refrain from conversations about:

Your work   Your children

Your in-laws   Money

333. Take walks after midnight.

334. Look up the definition of *romance* in the dictionary and try to understand all that real romance incorporates.

335. Get new lighting in your dining room so that you have a very soft, romantic atmosphere.

336. Have a contractor remodel your bedroom and put in a fireplace.

337. Give her a diamond friendship ring to show her that you think of her as your lover and as your friend.

338. Create your own fortune cookies by inserting personal, romantic fortunes into store-bought fortune cookies.

339. Buy her flowers from a street vendor on your way home from work.

340. Send a bouquet of white roses symbolizing that your love is pure and true.

341. Place a handsome silk tie in his briefcase before he heads off to a big meeting.

342. Get a pretty needlepoint pillow that says "tonight" and place it between the pillows on your bed.

343. Draw a little cartoon expressing your feelings for your mate.

344. Dress up in your best clothing for your next date or buy a new outfit. Dress to impress!

345. Brush her hair for her at bedtime.

346. Play hooky together from your careers, responsibilities, and the world.

347. Make her happy after a long day by preparing a candlelight bubble bath for her.

348. Have you had a major blowup? Try sending a dozen "I'm sorry" cards to your mate's office.

349. Fill her briefcase with love notes.

350. Take a vacation day off from work on Sweetest Day to enjoy it with your love or to plan a special celebration when she gets home from work.

351. When you dine out on your mate's birthday, always have a birthday cake brought to your table for dessert.

A smile is not only a woman's best cosmetic,
but it likewise serves as a non-verbal compliment
to her companion.
— DR. GEORGE W. CRANE

---

352. Send a roll of Life Savers with a note stating that your mate is your real-life lifesaver.

353. Have a "Significant Other Day" every few months when you simply spend the entire day relishing your relationship.

354. Take lots of photographs of you and your mate when you are on vacation and at other times when you are having extraordinary fun together. Let the pictures serve as happy reminders of these special moments together.

355. Keep a journal about your relationship and share it with your love.

356. Indulge his sweet tooth with an ice cream cake and be sure to have a sweet message written on top of the cake.

357. Give up watching soap operas on television—they are bad relationship role models.

358. To put yourselves in a mellow mood, get a CD of environmental sounds.

359. Does your love have the wintertime blues? Head to a warm, sunny place like:

Florida   Arizona

Hawaii   California

These climates should heal the blahs and warm things up between the two of you.

360. On a cold, dreary night, curl up together and read the works of Henry David Thoreau.

361. Be each other's best friend.

362. Give for the sake of giving. Don't expect anything in exchange for your gifts.

363. Love for love's sake.

364. Hide a piece of jewelry in a red Jell-O dessert and top it off with whipped cream.

365. Give a gift certificate to a perfume shop when you want to buy a present but feel unsure about what to buy.

366. Enjoy Candlemas Day (February 2) by having candles everywhere in your home.

367. Dye all your Easter eggs red instead of the usual pastel colors for a little touch of romance.

368. Never, ever gossip with your friends about your lover.

369. Strive to keep your relationship as tear-free as possible.

370. Stop saving romance for:

Holidays   Vacations

Anniversaries

371. Even if she just has a cold, always bring her flowers when she is sick.

372. Throw a coin into a fountain and make a romantic wish together.

373. Dress in a style that will be pleasing to your mate (at least once in a blue moon).

374. Plant a beautiful window box outside her bedroom window.

375. Make it a three-day weekend instead of the usual two-day version.

376. Give him your unlisted telephone number.

377. When you have absolutely no idea what to give her for a special occasion, take her on a New York City shopping spree to pick out her gifts from you.

378. Close the drapes, pull down the blinds, and put your imaginations to work.

379. Become parents of a different kind together by adopting a pet from an animal shelter.

380. Give her a good luck charm to carry on days when she is feeling a little down on her luck.

381. Always follow your heart.

382. Keep in mind that with arguments there are always three sides to the story:

Yours	Your partner's
The facts	Fight the fair fight.

383. Discover paradise hand-in-hand.

384. Never overschedule your couple time. You need time for spur-of-the-moment romance.

385. If you need a little help writing love letters, pick up a copy of Reader's Digest's *The Illustrated Reverse Dictionary*. It allows you to start with an idea and then leads you to words with that specific meaning.

386. Before your next getaway, send off for luggage tags and have your and your mate's pet names for each other put on the tags.

387. Want to feel like young lovers again? Try a getaway to Disneyland or Disney World.

388. Are you stuck in a romantic rut? Want to get his heart pounding wildly? Try:

Parasailing	White-water rafting
Sky diving	A roller coaster ride

A little adrenaline goes a long way toward promoting passion.

389. Send a May Day bouquet on May 1.

390. Take an old-fashioned Sunday afternoon drive to a scenic spot and enjoy this time to simply be together.

---

*A variety of nothing is better
than a monotony of something.*
—JEAN PAUL RICHTER

---

391. Use cute magnets to attach romantic cartoons and mementos to your refrigerator door.

392. Give him a personalized license plate for his new car. Contact the Bureau of Motor Vehicles to determine what initials are available.

393. Send a musical greeting card to your love. If possible, send one that plays "your song."

394. Buy your mate a fabulous new jewelry wardrobe and, for good measure, throw in a lovely jewelry box.

395. Work at keeping your love always growing and changing for the better.

396. Listen to Mozart tonight instead of hard rock.

397. Try to keep discovering the hidden little passions, likes, and dislikes of your mate.

398. Stop yourselves from going to bed angry with each other.

399. During difficult relationship times, try to remember why the two of you got together in the first place.

400. Only in an emergency, I repeat, only in an emergency should you break a date.

401. Are you thinking about him? Pick up the phone and tell him!

402. Seduce your mate tonight.

403. If you want passion to be a part of your love life, try being passionate.

404. Keep both of your passports current so that you can take off on a moment's notice to an exotic getaway.

405. Sing a duet with your love.

406. Place your jacket around her shoulders on a cool evening.

407. Hold a private conversation between the two of you in absolute darkness.

408. Three little keys to romance:
Secrets   Sexiness
Silliness

409. Hold her when she cries and wants to be comforted.

410. Throw a party and invite all the members of your wedding party.

411. Take good care of him when he is sick—yes, even if he is a big baby.

412. Learn the knack of being impractical.

413. Tell your mate what turns you on.

414. Develop a shared sense of wonder about your relationship.

415. When you write a love letter, try to make it thought-provoking and haunting.

416. If he suffers from a case of "blue Mondays," send him a cheer-up card at work each Monday.

417. Search out romantic settings in your area, such as:
Art galleries   Quaint cafés
Museum gardens   Scenic drives
The seashore   Mountaintops

418. Whenever you vacation, always make it a point to dine at a fabulous, memorable restaurant.

419. Give up trying to change your mate and start changing yourself.

420. Make a wreath out of red M&Ms for Valentine's Day. (Call the company at 800-627-7852 for instructions.)

421. Give her a new version of her favorite childhood toy.

422. Think of your love as a special gift from God. After all, it really is!

423. When you both need some rest, buy matching satin eye masks.

424. On a lovely summer night, sleep on your screened-in porch together.

425. If she won't tell you what she wants for Christmas, take her to visit Santa. Then ask the bearded gentleman what she said.

426. Carry a beeper so that you can always be in touch with each other.

427. Spend the holidays together in exotic locations.

428. Always treat your partner with respect. There are no exceptions here!

429. If he hates to shop for clothes, do it for him or send him a subscription to several men's clothing catalogs.

430. Give up the outdated notions of power and control in romantic relationships.

431. Rent a convertible for your next date on a pretty day.

432. Fill every one of her shoe boxes with little Valentines.

433. Buy her anything that is connected with feathers for a little touch of the exotic:
    A boa   Slippers
    A feather pen

434. For men only: Read *The Secret Language of Women* by Sherrie Weaver for a fun, offbeat guide to the gentler sex.

435. Love so that you don't have *any* regrets.

436. Walk the romantic walk. Talk the romantic talk.

437. Meditate together.

438. The number one relationship killer: taking each other for granted.

439. The number two relationship killer: putting up walls.

440. The number three relationship killer: not expressing your true feelings.

441. The number four relationship killer: being complacent.

442. Get out your parents' or grandparents' big band albums. Make a great tape of some wonderful dance music.

443. Plan a trip down California's Highway 1 for the most picturesque trip of your life.

444. Court each other on a daily basis.

445. Keep your teasing to fun topics (that means fun for both of you).

Men always want to be a woman's first love—women like to be a man's last romance.
— OSCAR WILDE

---

446. How about spending the evening going parking at a teenage make-out spot?

447. Thrill your significant other by surprising him with two round trip tickets on the Concorde from New York to Paris.

448. Hire a professional songwriter to write a song for your love.

449. Make a donation to your mate's favorite charity instead of giving a gift.

450. Always celebrate your lover's birthday (even the ones that your lover would rather forget).

451. When she suggests that you save money by not exchanging gifts for a special occasion, refuse!

452. Place the flowers he sends you in a place of importance in your home and where he will be sure to see them.

453. Keep in mind that romantic gestures always have a snowball effect on a relationship. They create more romance!

454. Rules for fabulous, romantic gift giving:
Make it expensive or extravagant
Be sure the gift will be highly desired
Give it at an unexpected time
Present it in an unusual manner
Don't let it be practical in any way, shape, or manner

455. Both of you should read the current bestsellers on relationships and then discuss them.

456. Attend a romance workshop together. Many churches are now offering relationship retreats, so check them out for a big help in improving the quality of your relationship.

457. Just for the fun of it, place a silk nightie in her briefcase so that she'll have some pleasant thoughts of you when she gets to her office.

458. Buy her a new outfit for your next evening out on the town.

459. Make a toast to your mate at your next party.

460. Visit all your friends and family who live in exciting locations for a low-cost getaway.

461. Stop putting off being romantic! Bring your mate flowers and candy tonight!

462. Stock up on your love's favorite junk food so that being with you will be even nicer.

463. Splurge on her dream car. How about a BMW or a Cadillac? For him, how about a Corvette or a Mercedes?

464. For a small touch of romance, sleep on satin sheets.

465. Focus on all the good things about your mate.

466. Make a lengthy list of all the blessings that are a part of your relationship. Start adding to the list on each anniversary and holiday.

467. Kiss at stop signs.

468. Kiss at red lights.

469. Kiss at railroad crossings when you must wait for a long time.

470. Frame the lyrics to a beautiful love song and give it to your love.

471. When she travels by air, always take her to the airport.

472. Decorate your love's Christmas gifts with:
    Mistletoe   Candy canes
    Special ornaments   Chocolate Santas
Remember that the presentation of a gift is almost as important as the gift itself.

473. Meet your lover at the door wearing a costume to liven things up just a bit.

474. Leave a trail of small chocolates for your love to follow and to find you waiting for him.

475. Drop the daily grind in favor of romance. Be a spur-of-the-moment kind of lover.

476. Never hold back when you are expressing your love for your mate.

477. Meet for an afternoon tea party at a grand hotel.

478. Ask your mate to give you a list of his favorite love songs. Put the list to good use.

479. Perfume all your love letters or write on scented stationery.

480. Get home earlier than your mate and meet her at the front door with a teddy bear and flowers.

481. Go fruity! Stop by a bath shop and pick up little bottles of fruit-scented gels and lotions for your love.

482. On evenings when she is too busy to do the dishes, furnish beautiful paper plates to use at the dinner table.

483. Validate your lover's feelings. Everyone wants and needs to feel understood.

484. Make a wise investment in the local job market and hire a sitter for your children so that you two can enjoy a night out.

485. Instead of going out, hire a sitter to entertain your children while the two of you enjoy an evening at home.

486. Start a little collection of all kinds of candles:
Tapers   Votive
Holiday   Scented

487. Place a tin of gourmet cookies in his briefcase before his next business trip.

488. Place a "Do not disturb" sign on your office door when your lover visits.

489. Have a little romantic fun of another kind. Play cupid for another couple.

490. Kiss him more often.

491. Wash her hair in rainwater.

492. Always take her telephone calls.

493. Carry her over all hotel thresholds.

494. Have personalized labels made for his liqueur or wine bottles. Try to add a touch of romance to them like a small heart in one corner.

495. Buy a mood-music CD. They are inexpensive and available at most discount stores and record shops.

496. Give her a gift certificate for maid service. We guarantee she'll like this one!

497. Present your mate with a blue ribbon for being the best lover.

498. Spend an evening together watching your old home movies to recapture the romance of earlier times.

499. Wrap her gifts in gifts. Use:
Scarves   Tablecloths
Placemats

500. Ask her friends what it would really take to impress her.

501. Kiss, kiss, kiss. Here is a list of reasons to kiss, as if you need any!
Kiss hello   Kiss of gratitude
Kiss with sexual innuendo
Kiss—just because!

502. Maintain strong ethical ideals about romance.

503. Cover a wall with photographs of the two of you. Use thumbtacks on a cork base to hang the pictures.

504. Can't get away for the weekend? Take a fun day trip.

505. Re-create your first meeting (even if it means a pilgrimage across the country) on the anniversary of your first meeting.

506. For a first-class night's sleep, order Egyptian cotton sheets for you and your love to enjoy.

507. Have a beautiful tea set handpainted for your tea-loving mate.

508. Feeling stressed out over an argument? Wind down together by listening to some jazz.

509. Throw the PERFECT party in honor of your mate.

510. Dress up her beloved pooch for the holidays. Go one step further and have the pooch bring her a gift. Be sure that the costume is safe and comfortable for Fido.

511. Pick up silly souvenirs of your travels together.

512. Always call when you tell your mate that you are going to call.

513. Treat her like a queen.
Treat him like a king.
OK, for at least a day!

514. Put a little touch of romance in the air—buy a bubble machine.

515. Fix a basket of homemade goodies for your significant other.

516. Memorize your favorite love poem.

517. Give a gift certificate from a lawn and garden center to your nature-loving mate.

518. For your anniversary, give her a fabulous new wedding band.

519. Try a touch of sensible romance. Give a month's or a year's worth of:

Lunches   Subway tokens

Parking

520. Ask your mate for his definition of commitment. To be a great couple, both of you must have the same idea of commitment.

521. Escape from the pressures of modern civilization with your mate.

522. Give your mate loads of attention and affection.

523. Celebrate the idea of Valentine's Day throughout the year.

524. Give up nagging your mate.

525. Come home early from work to take her to a romantic matinee.

526. Send a huge basket of nuts to her at the office with a note saying that you are nuts for her.

527. Have a special fragrance created just for her.

528. Send a pair of doves to your mate as a beautiful token of your love.

529. Create your own book of great romantic quotations and give it to your love on a special anniversary.

530. When you build your first home, write both of your initials in the freshly poured concrete driveway or patio.

531. When he gets a raise or promotion, send him a split of champagne at the office to enjoy at lunch.

532. When you are planning a romantic dinner, use your sense of smell, touch, taste, sight, and sound to create an unforgettable evening.

533. Purchase a set of brightly colored markers to make your love notes a work of art.

534. In the evenings, always keep your lights turned down low to set a romantic mood.

535. If he brown-bags his lunches, put yummy gourmet treats in his sack.

536. Place gifts in heart-shaped boxes for beautiful gift giving.

537. Trade love stories with other romantics. You can't ever have too much romance in your life.

538. Set the romantic standard among your peers.

539. Throw at least one party together a year.

540. Take the romantic lead in your relationship. Be assertive.

541. For men only, here is a little tip: Many women find talking to be the best type of foreplay.

542. Place oversize pillows in front of your fireplace for great late-night snuggle sessions.

543. When it comes to dating, be a good sport.

544. Tell her that it is your turn to:
Do the dishes   Change the baby
Clean the house
These statements will be beautiful music to her ears.

545. Sign your letters and cards with X's and O's (kisses and hugs).

546. Always compliment the cook.
Always kiss the cook.

547. Remember that two can dream bigger than one, so get your mate involved in planning:
Romantic gestures   Vacations
Getaways   Holiday celebrations

548. Arrange clandestine meetings all over town.

549. Give your mate a cuddly live bunny rabbit for Easter.

550. Place heart-shaped bookends on his bookshelf for a touch of romance.

551. Go on an old-fashioned romantic fall hayride.

552. Be the spark in your lover's eyes.

553. Instead of counting sheep when you can't sleep, count hearts.

Friendship consists in forgetting what one gives and remembering what one receives.

— DUMAS

554. Fly a heart-shaped kite on windy days and let the whole world know that you are a romantic.

555. Get some ESP going between you and your lover.

556. Share a bottle of unisex cologne that you both love.

557. Order a romantic dress or accessory for her from a mail order catalog.

558. Keep the celebration going by giving another present on the day after your mate's birthday.

559. Go all out for romance by building a heart-shaped deck or patio.

560. Stop taking phone calls from your ex.

561. Wait for her under the mistletoe.

562. Treat her to a gorgeous designer evening gown.

563. Send her an old-fashioned homecoming corsage before the big game.

564. When you aren't ready to use the word "love," try one of these:

Devotion	Regard
Respect	Warmth
Affection	

565. Try to be enchanting on your next date.

566. Invent your own little reasons to celebrate together.

567. Always remain true to your mate.

568. Use fresh flowers as you would use bows on presents.

569. For a change of routine in your kiss repertoire, try kissing your mate's neck, chin, forehead, or eyelids.

570. Always open car doors for her.

571. Send a cactus instead of the usual type of potted plant.

572. Tint your popcorn red for your Valentine's Day movie date.

573. Send a rosemary plant with a note saying that you will always remember:

Your mate	Last night
Your time together	Your wedding day

574. Celebrate the Summer Solstice (June 21) by going out to a summer festival.

575. Host a Valentine's Day tea in honor of your mate.

576. Ask your love to give you a list of her favorite meals and desserts. Next, get busy learning how to cook them.

577. Send your mate to a wonderful spa for a day, weekend, or week of pampering when you feel that she needs some extra TLC.

578. Fill his car with pink and red balloons.

579. To be a successful romantic, pay attention to the tiniest details when planning dates, vacations, and gift buying.

580. Keep in mind that the most romantic people are:

Playful	Whimsical
Lighthearted	Tenderhearted

581. Brighten your love's day by sending flowers for no reason. We guarantee that it will do the trick.

582. Give him a leather Bible with your names and wedding date inscribed on the cover.

583. Spend the night in a fabulous hotel in your own city for a romantic but easy getaway.

584. Wink at each other often.

585. Blow kisses to each other from across a crowded room.

586. Give two to five hugs to each other every single day—no exceptions, please.

587. Start snuggling and cuddling all over again.

588. Have an "Us" day:
> Plan your favorite pastimes
> Dine at your favorite restaurant
> Listen to romantic music
> Give a little gift to each other

589. Call every time that you are running late.

590. Take an afternoon nap together before a big night out on the town.

591. Choose the most beautiful engagement ring that you can afford. After all, she will have it for the rest of her life.

592. Give your love an old-fashioned friendship ID bracelet for a nostalgic touch of romance.

593. Try to come up with a new romantic idea each week and be sure to put it into practice.

594. Take her mother to lunch, and she and her mom will love you for your kindness.

595. Look to great, happy couples as role models for your relationship.

596. Feeling a little timid? Start small:
> Place his favorite candy bar under his pillow
> Put a romantic cassette in her Walkman
> Place a tulip on her pillow
> Give a McDonald's gift certificate for breakfast to a mate who never has time to eat in the morning

597. Set a beautiful table setting for each meal that you share with your mate.

598. Can't think of anything romantic to say? Just quote some of the best:
> William Shakespeare   John Keats
> Elizabeth Barrett Browning

599. Mail a suggestive but cute note to your mate at his office.

600. Express your feelings in your own unique style.

601. For a romantic surprise, replace all the sheets in the linen closet with satin ones or heart-motif ones.

602. Send a gigantic box of chocolates to your love at the office, where he can share the goodies with his coworkers.

603. Find a fancy alarm clock that will play a sweet tune to wake up your sleepyhead.

604. Remodel her office while she is out of town on an extended business trip.

605. When your wife first finds out that she is pregnant, give her a fabulous maternity wardrobe.

606. Have all her diamond jewelry cleaned for her by a trusted jeweler, and surprise her with a new piece hidden among the clean ones.

607. Let your neighbors know that you are one romantic guy by having a heart-shaped pool in your backyard.

608. Share a string of red licorice candy, and be sure to kiss when you get to the center of the string.

609. Lie on the summer grass side by side and watch cloud formations. What do you see? Look for hearts and cupids.

610. Ask your love out for Valentine's Day a few months in advance.

611. Buy him a dozen boxes of his favorite Girl Scout cookies. You will even make a scout happy with this one.

612. Plant a Christmas tree in honor of your first Christmas together.

613. The two best gifts for a serious relationship are:
     Time   Forgiveness

614. Visit the birthplace of the Bard and enjoy a romantic vacation at the same time. Take him to Stratford-upon-Avon, England.

615. At his next big birthday party, stand up and make a major tribute to him.

616. Nurture her spirit by creating beautiful surroundings for her.

617. Give a basket of fresh handpicked blueberries, strawberries, or blackberries for a little summertime gift.

He who makes a romantic gesture should never remember it and he who receives one should never forget it.
— AUTHOR UNKNOWN

618. Give a fabulous gift of a bright future by giving your mate a college education.

619. When the two of you leave on a romantic getaway, tuck a little collapsible bag in her suitcase to fill up with mementos of your trip.

620. To make your home seem more romantic, keep it tidy and pleasant.

621. If your mate has trouble remembering dates or runs late, give him a:

    Watch   Planner
    Calendar   Clock

622. At least one night a week go to bed together at 8:30 p.m.

623. Frolic in a waterfall or stream on a visit to a warm climate.

624. Get a small blackboard for your kitchen and leave little love notes on it.

625. Listen intently for her footsteps upon her homecoming.

626. Want to give your mate a needed and much appreciated gift? Try giving her a break!

627. Sit around a campfire and share stories about your past or feelings about your love.

628. Facing a bad day? Pull the covers up over your heads and stay home together.

629. Look at your wedding photographs as if you were seeing them for the first time.

630. Enroll in a flower-arranging class so that you can create your own floral masterpieces.

631. Give yourselves something different to celebrate:
Arbor Day
Fellowship Day
Groundhog Day
Loyalty Day
Children's Day
Poetry Day
Old Maid's Day

632. Watch a made-for-television romantic thriller together. Check out the programs on HBO and Lifetime.

633. Vow to please your mate *and* yourself.

634. Whenever you give a gift to your lover, buy the best one that you can reasonably afford.

635. Re-create an old-time dance party from days gone by. Be sure to include lots of songs to slow-dance to in your musical selections.

636. Strive to be interdependent, not codependent.

637. How about bringing sweets to your sweet:
Cobblers
Cookies
Custards
Napoleons
Eclairs
Glacés
Mousses
Puddings
Cakes
Pies

638. Share all your financial assets. Yes, we said *all* your assets.

639. Dress up in a fun costume to cook a holiday meal for her. Be:
Santa
Easter Bunny
Cupid

640. Surprise your mate by taking a chance on romance on Chance Day (August 7).

641. Love with dignity, grace, and style.

642. Believe that *you* are very lovable and you will be.

643. Great love = great risk.

644. At night, share your pillow with your lover.

645. Stop thinking of romance as work. Think of it as maintenance for a healthy relationship.

646. When her car is in the repair shop, provide your own personal taxi service for her. At the end of the day present her with your bill and ask her to pay it in kisses.

647. Before you retire to the bedroom for the night, lightly spray it with rose or gardenia air fragrance.

648. Give big bear hugs to your mate.

649. Simple rule of romance: Happiness is contagious.

Bonds of matrimony:
worthless unless the interest is kept up.
— AUTHOR UNKNOWN

---

650. Go on a spring break like you did as a teenager, but this time, turn it into a romantic spring break with your partner.

651. Allow your heart to fall deeply, madly, and wildly in love. Stop holding back.

652. When she reads a tragic love story, hand her a beautiful lace hankie.

653. Sign your mate up for a subscription to a romantic book club.

654. Secretly place your picture in her locket.

655. Fluff his pillows for him.

656. Start a romance club with other people who are true romantics and share your ideas about love, romance, and relationships.

657. Write a fan letter to your mate stating all the reasons that he is special to you.

658. Build a fabulous, heart-shaped sandcastle the next time you and your love go to the beach.

659. Make a wish together on a new moon for some great romance to come to you (wish over your left shoulder for best results).

660. Take a romantic ride in the Tunnel of Love at the next carnival you visit.

661. Sleep together like a pair of spoons.

662. When your mate gets passed over for a promotion, start a cheer-up campaign to raise his spirits.

663. Order room service for two and stay in your hotel room instead of venturing out on the town.

664. Dress up in a period costume and cook a meal from an antique cookbook.

665. Reserve the penthouse suite for your next business trip, and take your mate along.

666. Dry some flowers from all the bouquets he sends you to make a beautiful new bouquet that is filled with happy memories.

667. Snuggle under a heavy down comforter so that you'll feel as snug as two bugs in a rug.

668. Bake Valentine cookies together and deliver them to all your couple friends.

669. Strive always to make your mate feel valuable and worthy.

670. Keep a healthy mindset of:

Love	Joy
Happiness	Fun

671. Know that a trouble shared is a problem split in half. Help each other as much as you can.

672. Have a fun fight—a food fight in the kitchen.

673. Arrange to meet for a morning coffee break.

674. Give a foreign edition of your mate's favorite magazine, newspaper, or book for a little touch of the exotic.

675. Rent an RV and drive to all the towns and cities that have romantic names or attractions.

676. Buy Band-Aids with hearts all over them to give to your mate when she has a little accident.

677. Give her a new wedding gown for when the two of you renew your vows.

678. Try to obtain a foreign language version of "your song."

679. Change the lighting in your bedroom by placing an old-fashioned oil lamp on the nightstand.

680. Give her a matching set of cloth-covered boxes filled with all kinds of little romantic gifts. Hide the boxes in each of her closets throughout the house.

681. On Memorial Day weekend, sit down together and make a lengthy list of all the fun activities that both of you want to do during the upcoming summer months.

682. Be sure to make your dinner hour together a nice, quiet, calming time in your busy day.

683. Create boundaries (not walls) within the relationship to allow for personal freedom.

684. Allow extra time for your lovemaking.

685. Purchase some beautiful ribbons for her hair.

686. When she falls asleep tonight, tuck her favorite childhood toy in beside her to give her a heartwarming surprise when she awakens in the morning.

687. Make a heart out of brown sugar to top off his bowl of oatmeal (one of the few foods that the American Heart Association recommends for a healthy heart).

688. Get a pair of tropical fish for his office and name them for the two of you.

689. Promise her that she'll never have to be out in the dating world *ever* again.

690. Put these attitudes to work in your relationship:
Giving   Sharing
Caring

691. Buy a pair of his and her rockers for your porch or deck, and spend your evenings getting reacquainted.

692. Always lend a helping hand to your mate.

693. Give a set of wind chimes to create a wonderful sound of romance on breezy evenings.

694. For a lovely anniversary gift, have a beautiful oil painting made from your best wedding photograph.

695. Give a mini–back rub to your mate when she is stressed and working late at her desk.

696. Surprise your love by getting one of his love poems to you published in a poetry magazine.

697. Give her happy feet as part of her Valentine present by placing a pair of red Hush Puppies on her feet.

698. Create a deep and moving experience for the two of you to share. Take a romantic trip to one of the most scenic parts of the United States: Sedona, Arizona.

699. Try a little educational romance by visiting a planetarium and seeing a star show.

700. For every date that the two of you have had, send a chocolate kiss to him in the mail.

701. Realize that forgiveness is the end of an argument.

702. Reward all romantic gestures with words of appreciation.

703. Remember that you keep love by giving it away.

704. Affair-proof your relationship by:
Laughing together often
Making love regularly
Sharing your lives with each other

705. Give your mate your frequent flyer miles to use toward a fun getaway.

706. Be daring and parachute together in a double parachute.

707. Arrange for your mate to hear you saying nice things about him.

708. To improve the spiritual side of your relationship, attend a couples' Sunday school class.

709. Make some sacrifices for your lover. Start small, but significantly, by giving her more of the closet space.

710. Hide a diamond tennis bracelet in her tennis racket case.

Success in marriage is much more than finding the right person; it is a matter of being the right person.
— B. R. BRICKNER

711. Give him a set of personalized golf balls with your initials or other romantic symbols of your relationship.

712. Decorate your bedroom with floral garlands instead of bouquets.

713. When you come home from work, before asking, "What's for dinner?" tell your mate that you love her.

714. Never confuse your mate's role in your life with your parents' place in your life.

715. Rub wonderfully scented suntan lotion on her shoulders during a day at the beach. Another case of little things mean a lot!

716. Lavishly entertain his boss, friends, and family.

717. After an especially hectic week, spend the weekend reconnecting.

718. Give her the American dream—the house with the white picket fence around it.

719. When the telephone just won't do, buy a set of walkie-talkies to keep in touch.

720. Hire a topnotch furniture designer to create a wonderfully romantic bed for the two of you to share.

721. On the first night of summer, give your mate a beautiful set of patio furniture so that the two of you can spend more time under the stars.

722. Never suppress a compliment or a positive statement about your love. No one ever tires of hearing good things about themselves.

723. Keep in mind that true romantics are bold and brave. Love isn't for the timid.

724. Improve your romantic skills by reading a book on flirting.

725. Give tea towels, aprons, or potholders with hearts on them to her when you know that she is going to fix an extra-special meal for you.

726. Dine on heart-shaped dishes (available at most gift shops in early February).

727. Remember her beloved pooch on Valentine's Day with a heart collar or a red collar.

728. Give her a lovely pair of red gloves to keep her ring finger warm.

729. For women only: give him a week's worth of red gifts, such as:

Sunday	T-shirt
Monday	Muffler
Tuesday	Sweater
Wednesday	Tie
Thursday	Shirt
Friday	Robe
Saturday	Silk boxers

730. For men only: Give her a week's worth of red gifts, such as:

Sunday	Gloves
Monday	Umbrella
Tuesday	Shoes
Wednesday	Handbag
Thursday	Slippers
Friday	Robe
Saturday	Nightgown

731. Pick up some heart-shaped rolls or doughnuts for breakfast.

732. Never give up on your lover.

733. Propose on a national talk show.

734. Drink only red drinks on Valentine's Day:
Red wine	Cranberry juice
7Up with red food coloring	
Cherry wine coolers	Red Kool-Aid
Pink champagne	Pink margaritas

735. Attach a heart banner to your lover's mailbox.

There is a wealth of unexpressed love in the world. It is one of the chief causes of sorrow evoked by death; what might have been said or might have been done that never can be said or done.
— ARTHUR HOPKINS

---

736. Make an enemy of your lover's letter carrier by sending hundreds of love notes at one time.

737. Before a trip abroad, hide the appropriate foreign currency in your mate's passport to help in her big shopping spree.

738. Replace all her boring manila files with red, pink, and heart-covered ones to spice up her filing system.

739. Make a slide presentation for your love of all your trips together.

740. Make your own family heirloom by giving your love a piece of estate jewelry.

741. To keep the flame burning bright, get lots of firewood at the beginning of the winter season.

742. Have a powder room or bedroom mirror etched with:
Both of your initials	Your favorite poem
"Your song"	

743. Plant flowers, bulbs, or a tree on your anniversary.

744. Make up a secret code and write a love letter to your mate. Let your mate have fun trying to decipher it.

745. Collect all your love letters, love notes, and cards, and have them bound into a leather book.

746. Tonight share a sauna and get all "steamy" together.

747. Turn a picture into a classic treasure by hiring a photographer to take black-and-white photographs of the two of you and then framing the best one in a sterling silver frame.

748. Always see her safely home after a date.

749. Purchase matching Valentine's Day pillowcases and use them throughout the year.

750. Need a little escape, but you don't have time? Have a gourmet picnic on the fire escape of a high-rise building.

751. Spend the night together in a child's tree house.

752. Give your love a copy of *2002 Things to Do on a Date* and ask her to mark all the ideas that appeal to her.

753. Teach her dog to present her with the flowers you brought home from the florist.

754. Have cocktail napkins printed with:
　　Your anniversary date
　　Both of your initials
　　Your first date anniversary
　　The date of when you met
　　The date of the day you proposed
Use them often as happy little reminders of your relationship.

755. Keep in mind that your love will be thrilled (and relieved) when you take the romantic lead.

756. Know that your mate wants you to be romantic.

757. Leave more than one message on her answering machine. Make each message more romantic than the previous one.

758. Use your computer to print up romantic:
　　Coupons　　　　　Junk mail
　　Form letters　　　Invitations

759. Romantic tip: You will change and your mate will change. Therefore, your relationship will change. The trick is to make sure that all the changes are in a positive direction.

760. Schedule a make-out session for this week.

761. When you feel tongue-tied, let a poem title, song title, or book title express your feelings.

762. Whenever you travel together, call it a honeymoon.

763. If you simply can't write a good love letter, get a trusted friend to do it for you. Just be sure to swear him to secrecy or your name will be MUD.

764. Rent a large commercial sign for your love's front yard and put a love note on it.

765. Figure out how much you normally spend on your hobbies, sports, and personal interests for one month. Take that amount of money and spend it on romantic things instead. We guarantee that it will make a huge difference in your life.

766. Be very bold—throw a surprise wedding for you and your love.

767. For a night or a weekend, just pretend that you and your significant other are stranded on a deserted island.

768. Create a romantic flag of your own design and fly it in front of her house.

769. Start a collection of Department 56 Snow Village houses for her and choose buildings that will hold special meaning for her, such as:
   The honeymoon hotel
   The wedding chapel

770. Look for ways to break your "standard date rut." Routines lead to boredom in a relationship.

771. Send her a gorgeous Waterford writing instrument to use in her correspondence with you.

772. Give her a bride figurine for your anniversary.

773. Sign her up for the bridal registry at her favorite store and give her one of the gifts that she most desires.

774. Create an Easter tree for her with little egg ornaments and use a lovely strand of pearls as a garland on the tree.

775. Always send a greeting card in advance of every holiday so that your love will have longer to enjoy the card.

776. Make your home a wonderful place to come home to in every single way.

777. Right now, make up a list of five little romantic gestures that you can do for your mate in the next few weeks. Yes, you have to do them. Just writing them down is not enough!

778. Exercise your lips—kiss your lover.

779. When he is putting in too many long hours at the office, send him a vintage bottle of Cognac with a note telling him to come home to unwind.

780. Cover a dart board with photos of your old lovers. Next, let your mate practice his dart-throwing skills.

781. Spruce up your bedroom. Get a new gorgeous bedspread and drapes.

782. Decorate your bedroom like the honeymoon suite at your favorite hotel.

783. Always kiss and make up after a fight.

784. Here are the keys to handling your differences:
Learn from them   Embrace them
Enjoy them

785. Before jumping out of bed in the morning, do some stretching exercises together.

786. Close your eyes for 30-second intervals throughout the day and think good things about your mate.

787. Hang a Yuletide kissing ball in your foyer and put it to good use. Pucker up!

788. Looking for the perfect gift for your mate? Put a bow around your neck. Voilà!

789. Fix a delicious, romantic, late-night drink. Make a maple cider toddy:

> 2 cups cider (apple works best)
> 1 to 2 tablespoons maple syrup
> 1/4 vanilla bean, split
> 1/2 cinnamon stick (for garnishing)
> 6 allspice berries
> 1/2 cup brandy
> Combine all ingredients but the brandy. Simmer for 20 to 30 minutes. Strain the liquid. Add the brandy. Serve in front of a roaring fire or in bed.

790. For your pizza-loving mate, order an exotic flavor of pizza and share it under the covers on a cold evening.

791. Be her best cheerleader.

792. Give her a catalog and gift certificate from Gump's of San Francisco. The jewelry and gifts are the kind of thing that dreams are made of!

793. Stop believing that romance has to cost you a small fortune. The best things in life are free:

> Kisses   Hugs
> Whispers of sweet nothings

794. Get her in the mood.

795. Plan a relaxing vacation where you simply stay at home and do nothing, but you do nothing together.

796. When you are out to dinner, tell the waiter that you are on your honeymoon and receive better service and a touch of romance.

797. Become a passionate person, not just about romance but about every aspect of your life. You will be so much more attractive to your mate.

798. Purchase a color printer for your computer so that you can make banners, invitations, coupons, and cards.

799. Every time that you send flowers or bring candy to your mate, make it a different kind.

800. Learn the art of just being together in silence. It is a hallmark of all great couples.

801. Fill your bedroom with dozens of bouquets.

Reprove a mate in secret, but praise him before others.
— AUTHOR UNKNOWN

802. Arrange to be the vocalist at a wedding in the near future. Before the ceremony begins, tell your love that, in your heart, you will be singing the song to her.

803. Browse through a beautiful bridal department to feel like a bride all over again and to get yourself in a romantic frame of mind.

804. If you are thinking of buying a diamond engagement or anniversary ring, call DeBeers for an informative brochure.

805. Give a gift of romance and style by presenting your love with some wonderful designer candles.

806. Send a flower that holds special meaning in the world of flowers. Give your love camellias, which in Victorian days signified beauty. Be sure to tell her their meaning.

807. Float rose petals in her bath water.

808. Place a tiny yet elegant nosegay at her place setting at dinner tonight.

809. When you know in your heart that you have found your special someone, make a spur-of-the-moment marriage proposal.

810. Take a sunset harbor cruise together. Enjoy this beautifully romantic moment.

811. Serve heart-shaped cheeses for an appetizer.

812. Arrange a second honeymoon at a French or Italian villa.

813. Use a zillion candles as a romantic centerpiece.

814. Give an aromatherapy lamp to add wonderful fragrances to your home.

815. Order a zany but romantic Smitten Mitten. It is a double glove so that couples can hold hands but still keep the glove on.

816. Give a gift made out of velvet, such as:
Dress   Robe
Pillow

817. Send a beautiful antique Valentine to your lover.

818. Refinish an old steamer trunk and give it to her to use as a hope chest.

819. For an international touch of romance and style, give a box of French or Belgian chocolates.

820. Collect sterling silver heart charms and make a beautiful charm bracelet with them for your love.

821. Believe in love at first sight.

822. For a Victorian touch of romance, give her pearl:
Buttons   Comb and brush sets
Handled flatware

823. Send a darling sweet pea bouquet for a midweek pick-me-up.

824. Make a cassette tape of all the music that was played at your wedding. Play it to bring back wonderful memories.

825. Start nesting together.

826. Present her with an antique dance card before you take her out for an evening of dancing.

827. Are you having an incredibly busy workday? E-mail your mate instead of phoning her.

828. Name your home or apartment with the help of your mate. Choose a romantic type of name.

829. Invite your lover for lunch in the private dining room at your place of employment.

830. When your love arrives at the airport from an extended trip, have a band waiting at the gate to play "your song."

831. Bring exotic, lovely flowers back to your mate when you travel alone.

832. Before a big date, call your love from your car phone just to say that you are looking forward to your time together.

833. Propose all over again. Repeat the proposal down to the smallest of details.

834. Call him from the phone on the airplane when you travel without him, just to let him know that you miss him.

835. Make an event of dinner by making it a pink/red romance meal,

Use:	*Serve*:
Red table linens	Cranberries and ham
Pink dishes	Strawberries jubilee
Red and pink floral centerpiece	Pink champagne

836. Place a new sterling silver bookmark in the most romantic part of the book she is reading for her to find.

837. Give your bride-to-be Martha Stewart's *Weddings* magazine to give her marvelous ideas about planning your big day.

838. The only number you will need when it comes to fine chocolates: 1-800-GODIVA.

839. Replace your chrome doorknobs with beautiful floral ones for a lovely touch in the bedroom.

840. Give her a wonderful Limoge collectible, such as a:

Hatpin	Brooch
Button	Lady pin

841. For a getaway that you will never forget, travel to London and stay at one of the wonderfully romantic little hotels.

842. Search through flea markets and antiques shops and shows to find a lovely antique silver bride's basket to give to her for your anniversary or wedding gift.

843. Take your lover to one of the most romantic spots in the United States—Nantucket Island. Check with your travel agent for the most romantic inns.

844. Buy her a spectacular bauble from a well-known jeweler like Tiffany's or Harry Winston.

845. Cut a heart on the top of his steak before you throw it on the grill.

846. Compose a sonnet about all the time you have spent with your love.

847. Kiss goodnight at the front door (even if you are married).

848. Have a talented dressmaker create a miniature version of her wedding gown and present it to her in a shadow box.

849. Take your wedding picture to your florist and have them copy her bridal bouquet in silk flowers to present to her on your anniversary.

850. Before she arrives at your hotel room, decorate it in a romantic style.

851. Send a bouquet of state flowers from your lover's home state.

There is as much greatness of mind in acknowledging a good turn, as in doing it.
— SENECA

---

852. To feel like young lovers again, spend the weekend at your old college dorm.

853. When you shop with your mate, remember what he liked. Later, go back and stock up on future gifts for him.

854. Invite your mate to have dinner with you at every restaurant in town. If you live in a large city, prepare yourself for one major dining-out bill on your credit card!

855. Slip into the boardroom where she works before her big presentation, just to wish her good luck and give her a little kiss.

856. Look at your lover through rose-colored glasses.

857. Keep in mind that true romantics never confuse lust with love.

858. Share the covers. Yes, cover stealing can ruin even the best romantic night together.

859. Always treat her like a lady.

860. Even if you hate his taste in clothes, give him the freedom to choose without your well-intentioned interference.

861. Give a huge box of romantic CDs, movies, and books to a lover who is stuck at home. Gift-wrap each item separately and wrap the outside box.

You have to stay awake to make
your dreams come true.
— AUTHOR UNKNOWN

---

862. Take good care of your ladylove while you are out of town, by giving her a gift-wrapped box of self-protection presents:

Whistles	Door locks
Sting spray	Alarms

Enclose a note stating that you care what happens to her and want her to feel safe and loved.

863. Give her a CD single of "I Finally Found Someone" by Bryan Adams and Barbra Streisand.

864. When you are going to be out of town on business, send your shopaholic mate to New York City with a friend and have gift certificates set up at some of the wonderful shops along Fifth Avenue and 57th Street. That way she won't miss you as much.

865. As you drive home from work, shift gears in your head from business to romance.

866. For men only: Be sophisticated, be debonair, imagine that you are the James Bond of romance.

867. Spend this weekend at a secluded hideaway. Yes, we said *this* weekend.

868. Give your lover every reason in the world to trust you.

869. Romantic words to get into your vocabulary *and* your thoughts:

Boudoir	Fantasy
Exotic	Passion
Escapes	Intimacy
Ardor	Chivalry
Rendezvous	Monogamy
Honeymoons	Love

870. Be her earthly rock.

871. Give your mate lots of quality time.

872. Give your lover a tube of lip gloss after a long night of smooching to soothe her tired, chapped lips.

873. When you aren't feeling the least bit romantic, give her a set of Harlequin or Silhouette books for a touch of fictional romance.

874. Put gallantry to the test. Throw your coat down over a puddle to prevent her feet from getting wet.

875. At a large party, spend at least part of the time with your mate.

876. Always treat your mate like a date.

877. If you want to have a charming getaway, get Country Living travel service to plan it for you, because they have the largest selection of country inns and B&Bs in the United States.

878. Stop by the post office in early February for a selection of boxes, stamps, and cards with a romantic theme. Who would have thought that even Uncle Sam is romantic!

879. Give your love a Victorian-style rocker for nights when the baby can't sleep.

880. Present your love with tickets inside a beautiful handbag to a spectacular charity event.

881. Give her a gift that will make her the envy of all her friends.

882. Carve a cupid on your Halloween pumpkin instead of a scary face.

883. Wrap your presents in such a way that your mate won't be able to guess what is inside the box. Remember, surprises are romantic.

884. Find a hobby or pastime that both of you can share.

885. Grow old together, but always keep getting younger at heart.

886. Ditch your beepers and grab some quality private time together.

887. Talk to each other about your trouble spots first, before going to your in-laws and friends.

888. Always stand up for your mate with your family and friends.

889. Tell her that she is pretty. Women love to hear this!

890. Let bygones be bygones if you want to have a healthy, happy relationship.

891. Serve laughter and love with all your meals.

892. Throw a surprise anniversary party for your mate.

893. Make a list of all the ways that you and your love can create more intimacy in your relationship.

894. Keep in mind that one major component of a quality relationship is the ability to communicate. Spend time sharing:

Thoughts	Experiences
Goals	Dreams
Philosophies	

895. Fix a bulletin board where you tack mementos of your relationship. Place it where the two of you can see it every day and add more souvenirs of happy events.

896. Play date roulette. Make a list of twenty date ideas and place them in a jar. The next time the two of you are stumped for what to do, pull out a date from the jar and do it.

897. Take good care of your hearts:
No smoking   Exercise
Eat right   Get checkups
Stay in love

898. Commission a famous artist to paint her portrait. She will be so flattered.

899. Dance outdoors to the radio or a portable CD player on a beautiful night.

900. When you travel, look for hotels, B&Bs, and inns that have fireplaces in the bedrooms.

901. If your lover loves tea or coffee, go out and buy a dozen new flavors. This will be a nice little breakfast treat.

902. Make a list of the rooms in your home. Now make a list of one item that you can buy for each room that will make it more romantic.

903. For your chocolate-loving mate, create coupons good for fudge, cakes, brownies, and cookies that you will make when he redeems the coupons.

904. Shake things up a bit by:
Coloring your hair
Wearing a new style of clothing
Rearranging the furniture

905. Plan activities that give you both a feeling of being connected.

906. Give your love a copy of *Rebecca* by Daphne du Maurier to read. It is a wonderful gothic romance.

907. Stop playing games with each other. Honesty really is the best policy.

908. Check out America Online for lots of shopping and gift-giving ideas.

909. Give her a copy of one of the romantic Disney movies:
Beauty and the Beast
Snow White
Cinderella

910. When you want to play solitaire, play the double version just so you two can still be together.

911. If you are married, don't even consider divorce as an option. Remember that you promised for better or worse.

912. Host a dinner for two in a greenhouse when all the flowers are in bloom.

913. Have a quilt made that depicts a scene or saying that holds a special meaning for both of you.

914. When he is sick, fix a basket of:

Movies	Newspapers
Magazines	Paperbacks
Snacks	

915. When you and your significant other see a movie that she loves and it is based on a book, send a copy of the book as a reminder of the good time that you shared.

916. Take an exotic gondola ride in Venice. Too expensive? How about a canoe ride around a pretty local lake.

917. Place Valentine-style decorations throughout your home on your anniversary.

918. Give a tin filled with heart-shaped cookie cutters.

919. Get matching his and her pets. We have male and female golden retrievers.

920. Hold hands while doing scary stuff like riding on a ski lift.

921. Take a train trip together.

922. Sit in the back row of a movie theater and smooch during the slow parts of the movie.

923. Know the meanings behind the different colors of lingerie:

White—purity	Red—sexy
Black—sophisticated	Pink—sweet
Blue—serene	

924. Give a big bag of red M&Ms, which stands for romance.

925. Always sign your love letters in red ink.

926. Give a week's worth (seven different kinds) of cologne to your lover.

927. Take her to the spectacular Château Frontenac Hotel in Quebec City.

928. When good things happen for your mate, give him a sincere, loving pat on the back.

929. Be sure that he has a red or heart-motif tie to wear on anniversaries, Sweetest Day, and Valentine's Day.

930. Preserve her wedding gown and veil for your daughter.

931. Wake him up with a big kiss.

932. Hold her after a bad dream.

933. Hide your gifts inside other gifts.

934. Give a heart-shaped key chain or other style that has a special meaning for the two of you.

935. Always tell your lover the whole truth, even if it is painful.

936. Start a collection of songs that have the word "Valentine" in them.

937. Never, ever have more than one lover at a time.

938. Use your lover's name only in good times, not during arguments, so that it will always be music to her ears when you say it.

939. Take care of your own needs so that you won't be a burden to your lover.

940. Get him a big-screen television to watch his ball games on and keep him company for the really big games.

941. Make "happily ever after" your reality.

942. Break the world record for kissing the longest.

943. Kiss her twice before you leave for work in the morning.

944. When you need to put stars in your lover's eyes, give him a telescope to view the galaxy. Hopefully, some of the wonder and romance will rub off on him.

945. Give her an antique enameled box for a little anniversary gift.

946. Send a floral wreath instead of flowers. Ask the florist to hang it on her door.

947. Put little romantic requests in his office, home, and briefcase, asking for:

Hugs	Kisses
Snuggling	Pillowtalk
Dates	

948. Always pull out her chair for her when she sits down at a table and when she gets up from the table.

The test of a happily married and a wise woman is whether she can say, "I love you" far oftener than she asks, "Do you love me?"
— DOROTHY DAYTON

---

949. Place a tin of gourmet treats under the bed for yummy late-night snacks.

950. Literally become her knight in shining armor. Go to a costume shop to rent a suit of armor. Why not ride up to her front door on a white horse while you are at it.

951. Give her total control of the remote control for a week and you will see a lot more romantic programming.

952. Fly a flag of his favorite team on the day of an important game. Let him know that you share his enthusiasm.

953. Be the first one to suggest a smart, loving compromise to your problem.

954. Tuck a love note in his p.j.s.

955. Place a greeting card in his lunch bag.

956. Have a pillow fight at bedtime.

957. Tell your mate that he is fun to be with.

958. Place a heart by your name when you sign your cards and letters.

959. Stop an elevator between floors and have a mini-make-out session.

960. Squeeze into a photo booth together and capture your mugs on film.

961. Write a love story together.

962. Stop trying to be like the Joneses in the romance department. Learn to be comfortable being yourselves.

963. Give her a gorgeous lace apron when you know that she is planning a special dinner for the two of you.

964. Make love in every room of your house or apartment (hallways, attics, and large closets count).

965. Share your "I've always wanted to" stories. It could be that your mate feels the same way.

966. Show pride in your lover's accomplishments.

967. When you bring breakfast to your mate in bed, make a grand production of it. Have a tray, flowers, good dishes, and the morning paper.

968. Stop all the competition between you and your mate.

969. Learn to use friendly persuasion on your mate instead of ugly ultimatums.

970. Slip out early on your next meeting, party, or sporting event just to spend some time with your significant other.

971. Fix smores in the fireplace on a winter's evening and just chat about your lives, love, and dreams.

972. Plan a vacation months in advance to give yourselves something fun to look forward to together.

973. Always laugh at your love's jokes (even the bad ones).

974. At least once a month, do something nice for your mate, but don't let him know that you are the one who did it.

975. Place a beautiful Baccarat carafe by her bedside with a note saying that she is the water to your soul.

976. Give a practical mate a romantically practical gift, such as:
Securities   Mutual funds
Real estate   Stocks
For the romantic part, give ones that have a romantic link to them.

977. Place little love ads in every newspaper in your city declaring your love for her. If your love gets embarrassed easily, use your pet names for each other.

978. Give him a home theater system filled with romantic movies.

979. While she is away on a business trip, make some romantic changes to your home.

980. Allow time for your love for each other to deepen and become stronger.

981. Act on your romantic impulses to create passionate memories.

982. For a little lunchtime treat, take a yummy box lunch over to your mate's office and share your lunch hours.

983. Book a Valentine's Day or Sweetest Day overnight at a grand hotel or a quaint inn.

984. Have your florist design a lovely heart-shaped topiary for your love's desk or mantel.

985. Know the true "friends" of romance:
Baby-sitters   Mad money
Good timing   Holidays
Trips

986. Learn the difference between being romantic and being too romantic for your own good.

987. For men only: Give up your macho demeanor.

988. Wish your lover sweet dreams at midnight.

989. Fact: Optimists have better love lives than pessimists. Get our point?

990. Make use of daily affirmations to make yourself more romantic and a better mate.

991. Give your mate a pretty jar of green jelly beans.

992. Put a touch of lace around your home for a more romantic feel:

| On pantry shelves | On pillowcases |
| On towels | On placemats |

993. Take up a relaxing pastime where the two of you can enjoy the activity but still visit with each other:

Pasta making	Horseback riding
Herb gardening	Fishing
Antiquing	Canoeing
Backpacking	

994. Buy a tablet of Post-it Notes and use them to write tiny love notes.

A successful marriage is an edifice that must be rebuilt every day.
— ANDRÉ MAUROIS

---

995. Send your lover a scrapbook filled with memorabilia from your relationship.

996. Use doilies for a tiny touch of romance when you serve cookies, muffins, or candy.

997. Fill her hope chest with lovely, dreamlike gifts.

998. Always give Christmas/Hanukkah gifts to your lover.

999. Turn Valentine's Day into a huge holiday that both of you look forward to celebrating each year.

1000. Be a "middle mate." Have:
Middle-of-the-week dates
Middle-of-the-day dates
Middle-of-the-night dates
A midyear date

1001. Get friends to help you in the romance department:
Chauffeuring   Catering
Surprising

1002. On big birthdays, use the candles that refuse to get blown out and ask your lover to keep making romantic wishes.

1003. Give the cook a break, by bringing home dinner and spending the time together instead of one of you slaving away in the kitchen.

1004. Make love in front of a roaring fire.

1005. In February, it is easy to find lots of newspaper articles on relationships, love, and gift giving. Send any appropriate articles to your lover to get him thinking about romance.

1006. Learn to surprise your mate in ways that don't cost you anything:
An unexpected kiss or hug
A hidden love note
Singing to your love

1007. Whenever you travel on business, try to bring a little trinket back for your lover.

He who marries might be sorry.
He who does not will be sorry.
—Czechoslovakian Proverb

1008. Give your love a beautiful box of stationery with hearts or roses on it.

1009. Replace all the books in your den with:
Romance novels   Books of poetry
Relationship self-help books

1010. Make arrangements with the airline to have a gift brought to your love with her meal. She'll be the envy of all her seatmates.

1011. Take a midnight ride in the country on a hot summer's night.

1012. Instead of just dancing one dance at a dance or reception, make it a priority to dance every dance with your love.

1013. Send to her a new nightie every Friday for a month.

1014. Make scrolls out of your love letters. Write your thoughts on a heavy stock paper and then roll and tie them with pretty ribbons.

1015. Call your florist and ask what is the rarest flower that is currently in stock. Send a bouquet of these blooms with a note saying that your love for each other is rarer and more precious than the flowers.

1016. When you send a love letter to your mate's office, be sure to mark it "personal and confidential."

1017. Hang a lovely gold necklace on her car mirror and wait for her to find it when she starts her car.

1018. If you were high school sweethearts, get dressed up in your old prom clothes and spend the evening dancing to your old music.

1019. Pretend that you don't even know each other and try to pick each other up.

1020. Ask your fraternity or sorority members to serenade your love.

1021. Ask your best friend to plan a mystery date for the two of you and then call your mate with an invitation to the mystery date.

1022. If you don't have time to write a long love letter, send a love note.

1023. Compose new lyrics to "your song." Sing it to your mate on a karaoke machine to get the best effect.

1024. Give a darling CD house to her filled with romantic music.

1025. Before you leave on a business trip, mail a "missing you" card that will arrive on the day you leave town.

1026. Some suggested occasions to give your lover a gift:
> Your mate got a promotion
> Your mate had a really bad day
> Your mate got fired (a really, really bad day)
> Your mate had lunch with an old flame
> An old flame called your mate
> Your mate's best friend got a divorce
> Your mate's best friend got a huge promotion
> There is a new store in town
> There is a new florist in town
> Your mate did you a big favor

1027. When your love goes on a business trip, buy her a new cosmetic bag and fill it with travel-size soaps and lotions.

1028. Instead of picking your mate up at the airport as planned, surprise him by showing up at his hotel and arrange to stay together one more night. This idea takes some planning to pull it off. Check with your lover's boss to arrange the day off for her, change the airline ticket departure date, and be sure that this will work with her business schedule.

1029. At an old-fashioned soda fountain, split a banana split.

1030. Make a gigantic greeting card out of an old movie poster. Pick one of your favorite love stories and then write a romantic message on the poster.

1031. Ask all her friends to write a one-line compliment about her. Frame them and give them to her when she is going through a rough time.

1032. Slip a framed picture of yourself in his suitcase the next time he is called out of town on business so that he won't forget you.

1033. Give a world-class gift such as a:
> Home   Car
> Vacation home   Show dog
> Yacht

1034. If you simply can't bring yourself to unplug the phone, at least use your answering machine to handle all calls that happen during romantic moments.

1035. If your mate loves to cook, give:
    A library of cookbooks
    Fine cookware
    Cooking lessons
Include a note saying that you want to cook something up later together!

1036. Pretend to be busy and then, at the last minute, surprise her with a fabulous dream date.

1037. For men only: Compliment her on her:
    Career   Appearance
    Clothing   Hair
    Cooking   Home decor

1038. For women only: Compliment him on his:
    Job performance   Appearance
    Car   Athletic ability

1039. Spend an evening looking through your wedding photographs together.

1040. Decorate your bedroom in your mate's favorite color.

1041. Give her a new mini-wardrobe of clothing, shoes, lingerie, and a handbag in her favorite colors.

1042. Learn to play the guitar or the piano so that you can perform some romantic songs for your lover.

1043. Pass on great romance. If you have a unique way to show that you care, share the tip with your friends.

1044. Hire a masseuse to come to your home and give you and your mate a great massage.

1045. Attend a concert in the park on a Sunday afternoon and arrange beforehand to have the band dedicate a song to your lover.

1046. Do you want to be extravagant and take your mate out for a memorable date, but your budget is tight? Instead of having dinner at an over-priced restaurant, have cocktails in the bar instead—and then take your lover back to your place for a fabulous home-cooked meal.

1047. Travel a cross-country trip and stay only at romantic hotels.

1048. To be a great lover, try to live in the moment, at least during romantic ones.

1049. Plan a "classy" date:
Dinner at a five-star restaurant
Ballet   Opera
Theater   Symphony

1050. Take your dog-loving mate to the best dog show of them all—the Westminster Dog Show in New York City—and arrange to give her a puppy after the big show.

The secret of a happy marriage is simple:
Just keep on being as polite to one another
as you are to your best friends.
— ROBERT QUILLEN

1051. Make a romantic gift out of beautiful needlepoint pillows or rugs.

1052. Hide a love note in his dinner napkin saying that you are the dessert course.

1053. How about a touch of sophistication for him? Give him an elegant smoking jacket along with some fine cigars.

1054. For a wonderfully fragrant gift, send a gardenia plant instead of flowers.

1055. Strive to be magnanimous (look it up if you need to).

1056. Frame prints from cities that you have visited together.

1057. Have a selection of "mood" sheets:
Flannels for cold nights   Florals for a pretty bed
Satins for romantic times

1058. Give him a wardrobe of new shirts and ties for each day of the week.

1059. Tell each other all about your times apart so that both of you will feel comfortable with each other's absences.

1060. Overlook each other's faults (OK, so, you don't have any, but don't look at his).

1061. Give a book of gift certificates to a movie theater with instructions that the coupons can be used only for romantic or foreign films.

1062. Pick a theme for her gifts, such as:
Pamper Day—cosmetics, lotions, and beauty treatment gift certificates
Career Day—work-related new wardrobe, briefcase, pen
Pet Day—puppy with all the trimmings
Hobby Day—accessories that tie in with her special interest

1063. Give her a "plot" of her diamond (call a jeweler who specializes in diamonds) so that she can always know that she has the right stone.

1064. Have a bouquet delivered by a special messenger.

1065. Send a lovely box of gourmet foods instead of candy.

1066. Decorate her birthday cake with edible flowers for a touch of elegance.

1067. Place a pair of satin slippers by her old, scruffy slippers with a note saying that she is your Cinderella.

1068. Hibernate together during a major snowstorm.

1069. Get into the habit of thinking about romance and love throughout your day. You have to really work at this at first, but after a couple of weeks it will become automatic to you.

1070. Keep a postcard scrapbook of all the cards you send to each other.

1071. Prepare a basket of pet toys for when she gets a new puppy or when her dog is sick. Remember that the way to a dog lover's heart is through her dog.

1072. Always thank your mate for a date. Stop taking each other for granted.

1073. Give your dog-loving mate an oil painting of his four-legged buddy.

1074. After a great movie or musical production that your mate loved, send a soundtrack CD as a way to show that you care.

1075. "Look" at your lover through your sense of touch.

1076. Present a height-challenged mate with a romantically decorated footstool to make it easier for her to get things out of closets and cabinets.

1077. Browse an art supply store to pick up unique gift finds such as a paint by number kit for two.

1078. Give your love a work of art that speaks to his soul.

1079. Shop for gifts for your mate while the two of you are on vacation. Later, for holidays, give these gifts and your mate will be very impressed.

1080. Spend Saturday morning in bed together instead of running errands.

1081. Give a *lifetime* supply gift of:
Candles   Dishes with roses or hearts
Satin sheets   Fine wine or champagne
Romantic art for the whole house

1082. For a change of pace, try giving unique, out-of-print romance novels. Search for them at specialized bookstores, book auctions, flea markets, and antiques shops.

1083. Bestow a twin gift on your mate. If your lover likes a certain item, purchase two of them.

1084. Before a big night out on the town, thrill her with a new cocktail dress and accessories.

1085. Paint her toenails for her.

1086. Instead of sending a bouquet of flowers, send a single orchid. It is a lovely, understated way to say you care.

1087. Bring her flowers for her hair. Ask your florist for tea roses or violets.

1088. On a hot summer day, braid your love's long locks of hair to keep her cool.

1089. Do a little research and give her the newest item in the world of fashion.

1090. Give up the notions that romance is:
    Too much work   For singles only
    For young lovers

1091. Hide a ring inside a lovely English enamel box.

1092. When you give a present:
    Make it something your mate wants
    Beautifully gift-wrap it
    Present it in an unusual way

The only reward of virtue is virtue; the only way to have a true friend is to be a true friend.
— RALPH WALDO EMERSON

1093. Strive to be young at heart again. It will help you to be more creative, and it is one of the best ways to keep romance alive.

1094. Give the gift of romantic lingerie:
    For men—silk robes, smoking jackets, p.j.s
    For women—gowns, robes

1095. Send a beautiful wedding anniversary cake to her at the office.

1096. Mail a restaurant gift certificate with a notation that it must be used by the two of you on your next "romance" anniversary.

1097. Keep in mind that one of the best ways to be romantic is to learn the fine art of etiquette. Read Emily Post or Miss Manners to learn all about the social graces.

1098. Reasons to put romance to work in your relationship:
    You will feel closer to your lover
    Your mate will feel loved
    Your mate will feel special
    It is fun
    Your relationship will improve
    It is sexy
    Great lovers are always romantic!

1099. Never use romantic gestures to get you out of the "doghouse." If you need to get out of trouble, use the words "I'm sorry" or "I was wrong." Romance is to add fire to your love, not to calm a temper.

1100. Give a timeless gift of love like:

A gold watch	Pearls
A cameo	An engagement ring
Monogrammed cuff links	An anniversary ring
A gold heart-shaped locket	

1101. If you gave her an engagement ring years ago and can now afford a more extravagant one, propose to her all over again with a new, dazzling ring.

1102. Dance the night away:

At home to the radio	Under the stars on your patio
At a nightclub	At a wedding reception

1103. Give your lover a gift from Tiffany's. Everyone loves those tiny blue gift boxes.

1104. Volunteer to work for her charity to show how much you care about her *and* her interests.

1105. Fix a French picnic that includes:

A loaf of bread	A good selection of cheese
Fine wine	

1106. Send a membership to a flower-of-the-month club so that she will have a year of lovely flowers to remind her of your love.

1107. Make up a reason to celebrate together this coming weekend.

1108. Enjoy your times apart instead of being "mopey" that you aren't together; that way you will bring even more to your times together.

1109. Give a romantic pep talk to an unromantic mate.

1110. Always be polite to each other. It is so simple and makes a world of difference in the quality of your relationship.

1111. Be your own version of Christopher Columbus and look for new romantic places that the two of you can explore.

1112. Plan a party where everyone brings stories or mementos of your relationship.

1113. Host a gigantic yard sale to get rid of all his ex's stuff. Use the money to buy stuff for the two of you.

1114. Together, seek out the:
      Unfamiliar   Unknown
      Unusual

1115. When you can't sleep, make love.

1116. Rub his temples when he has a headache.

1117. Hide fresh flowers in the washing machine to make even the most boring task a little bit romantic.

1118. Smooch during traffic jams (discreetly, of course).

1119. Give him more time and energy for romance by paying a handyman to do his chores.

1120. Set off fireworks each time you enter a new phase of your relationship, such as:
      Dating each other exclusively
      Getting engaged   Getting married
      Big anniversaries   Having a baby
      Falling in love all over again

1121. Good lovers are good listeners, so learn the art of listening:
      Remain still and quiet while your mate talks
      Refrain from telling your story—just let your mate talk
      Ask questions   Don't interrupt
      Lean forward   Keep your eyes on your mate

1122. Be sure to pull your own romantic weight in the relationship. In other words, you can't expect your mate to be romantic if you aren't.

1123. Treat every day like Thanksgiving and have a sense of gratitude about your relationship.

1124. Set up a scholarship fund in your lover's name if he is academically minded.

1125. If your mate suffers from a health concern, donate medical equipment to a hospital in her name.

1126. Let your guard down when you are together.

1127. Romantic environments are:
   Smoke-free   Pollution-free
   Stress-free   Clutter-free

1128. Celebrate birthdays and anniversaries with an attitude of fun, excitement, and extravagance.

1129. Stop your tit-for-tat thinking.

1130. Practice the law of least resistance in your relationship.

1131. Perform a selfless act for your mate just because you are a nice guy.

1132. Qualities of a topnotch lover:
   Spontaneous   Open
   Honest   Spiritual
   Vital   Kind
   Self-sufficient   Loving
   Joyful   Gentle

1133. Take your lover to Cumberland Falls State Park resort in Kentucky to view the romantic, natural wonder of rainbows by moonlight.

1134. Give a writing pen that has hearts all over it for your mate to use when addressing your wedding invitations.

1135. Encourage your mate's hobbies by giving little gifts:
   Tennis—apparel, balls, new racket
   Jogging—shoes, clothes, case of sports drinks
   Bowling—bag, ball, glove, gift certificates for lane time
   Painting—art supplies, lessons, smock
   Dogs—books on a particular breed, obedience class gift certificate, toys, leash, treats
   Reading—books, bookmarks, new reading glasses

1136. Give a subscription to a magazine that pertains to your mate's interests.

1137. Present her with a pretty Madame Alexander doll that relates to her favorite romantic heroine, like:
   Cinderella   Scarlet O'Hara
   Juliet

1138. Hide a lovely set of Limoge dessert plates in the dishwasher for her to find with a note saying that you loved dinner last night.

1139. Fill her desk with snacks for when she is too busy to meet you for lunch. We recommend little sweetheart cakes.

1140. Make her feel loved by checking on her when she is home alone on a dark and stormy night.

1141. If she didn't receive her ideal wedding gifts when the two of you got married, why not buy some of them for an unexpected "post-wedding party for two." We suggest:
Fine china   Sterling flatware
Crystal goblets   Lovely table linens
Beautiful serving pieces

1142. Even if you stay at home on New Year's Eve, make it a party for two and a big deal, by:
Dressing up   Playing lively music
Wearing party hats   Blowing horns at midnight
Throwing confetti   Sipping champagne
Kissing at midnight

1143. On Groundhog Day, if he sees his shadow, hibernate together for the rest of the winter.

1144. Dress in your green jammies and stay home to celebrate St. Patrick's Day.

1145. If your sweetheart is a mom, for Mother's Day send a gift that lets her know that you still think of her as a lover and not just the mother of your children.

1146. Replace the practical items in your home with elegant versions of them, such as:
Paper bookmarks—sterling markers
Plastic letter opener—sterling opener
Bic pen—Mont Blanc writing instrument
Cookie jar—crystal biscuit box

1147. On Thanksgiving morning, present her with a list of reasons why you are most grateful to have her in your life.

1148. Make it a "picnic day" by preparing a picnic for each meal and enjoying the feasts in three romantic locations.

The best way you can surprise a woman with an anniversary gift is to give her just what she wanted.
— ARBUTH ARUNDALE

1149. Savor the last night of summer by sharing a meal served outdoors.

1150. Surprise her with a private lingerie shower, but with a twist. Give her items that she would love to have on a cold winter night:

Flannel p.j.s	Bunny slippers
Chenille bathrobe	Wool sleep socks

Just be sure that all the items have a heart motif of some kind.

1151. If your love wears a uniform to work, buy her a new one of a different style and attach a note that says, "Our love never goes out of style."

1152. Remember the moment that you fell in love with your mate and write a love letter telling your love all about it.

1153. Just for one date, speak with a French accent because it sounds romantic and sexy.

1154. Be a sneak! When you are shopping at an outdoor fair or market, make a mental note of what your mate admires and split up and buy it. After the two of you get home, give it to your love for a welcome surprise.

1155. If your mate drives a bunch of miles, fill his car with items such as:

Maps	A blanket
A flashlight	Flares
Snacks	A compass
Love notes	A map back to your home

1156. Send her a subscription to *Victoria* magazine to add a touch of romance to her life.

1157. Use your connections to help your mate's career or social standing.

1158. Find out which title your mate prefers:

Significant other	Partner
Wife/husband	Better half
Lover	Boyfriend/girlfriend

1159. Tie bows with red ribbons around all the trees in your backyard and attach a love note to each before you host a patio dinner for two.

1160. Give her lots of heart-shaped pillows.

1161. Start collecting lovely candlesticks, as romantics can never have too many.

1162. Give a gift of the other precious metal—platinum.

1163. Share a yummy dessert.

1164. When you dine at an elegant restaurant, feed him a taste of your dinner even though you want to savor each bite.

1165. Ways to tell if *you* are a true romantic:
> You celebrate "unusual" anniversaries
> You call for "no" real reason
> You look forward to Valentine's Day
> You have lingerie instead of p.j.s
> You have lots of candles in your home
> You write love letters
> You have sent a greeting card in the last few weeks
> You plan dates

1166. Romantics know that all couples have periods of closeness and then periods of moving away from each other. It is like a couple dance, and the trick is to hang in there during the moving away periods.

1167. If you love her name and you had better or you will be in deep trouble, monogram all kinds of gifts for her:

Towels	Shirts
Stationery	T-shirts
Tote bags	

1168. In love and life, it is perseverance that makes a huge difference.

1169. Sometimes, less is more. Give one fabulous gift instead of several small gifts.

1170. Spray a touch of cologne in his car before he leaves on a road trip as a subtle reminder of your relationship.

1171. Clean out your lover's closet and hang some new garments in with her clothing.

1172. For a mate who is a shoe lover, give a wardrobe of new shoes.

1173. Change:
    Your routines   Your usual holiday plans
    Your dating habits
Change is good!

1174. Dance together to the latest hit CD of romantic music.

1175. When you won't be spending the night together, give her a beautiful bed jacket to keep her warm.

1176. Encourage your love to go after her dreams. Help her achieve them.

1177. Three nice words that will make a big change in her attitude for the evening: "I'll cook dinner."

1178. Rent the offbeat but wonderful love story *Regarding Henry*.

1179. Go to a confectionery and ask them to make a special treat for your love.

1180. Fix a vending machine for your lover that gives coupons instead of treats. Write your own coupons like these:
    Good for a kiss
    Valid for a batch of homemade cookies
    Good for a hug
    Valid for a back rub

1181. Draw hearts on your envelopes.

1182. Order a set of bar glasses with both of your initials on them.

1183. Give your car-loving mate some new hubcaps and enclose a note saying that his love makes your world go around.

1184. Create a heart-shaped goldfish pond for your garden.

1185. Head to a fun culinary shop to buy every utensil, gadget, and pan that is heart-shaped.

1186. Make your bed together. Who knows where that will lead!

1187. Buy matching:
Jogging suits   P.j.s
Robes   Ski outfits
T-shirts

1188. Add red food coloring to the water and use an ice tray with heart shapes to make some romantic ice cubes.

1189. Don't set a romantic table for two. Instead set a beautiful table for one and then wait on your lover at dinner.

1190. Give a box of delicious chocolate-covered cherries or strawberries. So yummy!

1191. Make a batch of Rice Krispies Treats in the shape of teddy bears and put red icing hearts on them. Serve to your mate.

1192. Give a second chance to your first marriage (while you are still married)!

1193. Hold hands in public. Come on, be romantic. You can do it!

1194. Plan on growing old together.

1195. Never compare one relationship to another.

1196. Place a mistletoe wreath on your bedroom door.

1197. Read this book together and highlight ideas that you both love.

1198. Know that romance should be an acknowledgment of love, not confused with love.

1199. Take a romantic hot-air balloon ride together.

1200. Remember to build bridges and not walls.

1201. Give your lover a flawless diamond to represent your flawless love affair.

1202. Keep in mind that the act of caring is love in motion.

1203. Know that being in love should be an active rather than a passive pursuit.

1204. Ask her to dance even when the dance floor is empty.

1205. Call her the Queen of Hearts. Call him the King of Diamonds.

1206. Develop a strong sense of "we-ness" instead of "me-ness."

1207. Make her royalty, at least for a day. Take her to the palace at Monte Carlo.

1208. Free yourself from entanglements with old flames.

1209. Accept the fact that you must understand a person before you can truly love him or her.

1210. For men only: Know that married men live longer and have better health than single or divorced men.

1211. To save you and your lover from relationship disasters, admit when you are wrong.

1212. Have a relationship checkup once a month to talk about:
Any problems   Your feelings
What direction you want the relationship to take

1213. Celebrate the uniqueness of your relationship.

1214. Stop what you are doing whenever the two of you are alone and hear "your song" being played, and dance.

1215. Give three compliments to make up for every piece of criticism that you give your mate. Try not to give many criticisms.

1216. Send her a telegram when she is in the hospital and you are away on a business trip.

1217. Forgive your love for not being the perfect lover.

1218. Have a magician perform a new version of the "disappearing ring act." This time, though, have him produce an engagement ring for your lover.

1219. Hire a dance instructor to coach you both privately before your next big social gathering.

1220. Get a satellite system just because you want to watch more romantic movies.

1221. Ask a talented gardener to cut your shrubbery into heart shapes. (Try this in your backyard.)

1222. Throw an "unbirthday" party or an "it's not our anniversary" party for your lover.

1223. Ask him to a Sadie Hawkins dance for two.

1224. Once every year, give a major gift for no special reason other than romance.

1225. Call ticket agencies to obtain lists of upcoming events that your lover would enjoy.

1226. Arrange for both of you to get a leave of absence from work so that you can go on an extended vacation together.

1227. Turn Saturday nights into special events. After all, there are only fifty-two in an entire year, so you can't afford to squander them being couch potatoes.

1228. Everyone believes that romance is important before you get married, but we are telling you that it is even *more* important *after* you marry.

1229. Put Caller ID on your phone line so that you will always know when he calls.

1230. After you are married, take your mate out on the anniversary of your rehearsal dinner.

1231. Little ways to celebrate Valentine's Day:
Wear red
Send zillions of children's Valentines to your love
Give all types of Valentine candy
Give homemade cards
Give homemade goodies

1232. Be nostalgic about your relationship.

1233. Our "rules" for great relationships:

Be honest	Fight fair
Love unconditionally	Laugh often
Pray	Stay committed

1234. Take your love out to dinner to celebrate the good things that happen in his life.

1235. Install a hot tub in your home.

1236. Many people have replaced letter writing with E-mail or faxes, but there is nothing more romantic than receiving a love letter.

1237. We recommend having quality time, and we also recommend having lots of it.

1238. When she needs a lift, give her a piggyback ride.

1239. Take your love to a trendy bistro to celebrate an offbeat anniversary.

1240. Surprise him by showing up in a disguise when he is working late and dining alone.

1241. Sleep in a:
Four-poster bed   Brass bed
Twin bed (together)   Canopy bed

1242. Turn her dreams into a real-life wedding by getting married at the castle at Disney World. Check with your travel agent for details.

1243. Together, hold an unusual bonfire: Burn all your Rolodex cards with names of former lovers.

1244. Arrange to attend a prom together at your old high school.

1245. Stop complaining to your friends about the relationship. If you don't like something, take positive steps to change it instead of just whining about it.

1246. Have zillions of candles burning when she gets home from the office.

1247. Learn the art of empathy. In other words, imagine being in your mate's shoes.

1248. Fill a kitchen canister with heart-shaped candy and flowers.

1249. Give her a painting of the church where you were married.

1250. Expect the romantic best from your mate. In time, you'll get it!

1251. Hide a piece of chocolate inside her jewelry box beside her engagement ring.

1252. Have a "hot" summer night together.

1253. Rub scented lotion on her chapped winter hands.

---

*A happy marriage is a long conversation
that always seems too short.*
— ANDRÉ MAUROIS

1254. Take lots of romantic chances. After all, love isn't for the faint-hearted.

1255. For more privacy, travel during the off-seasons.

1256. Give her a romantic fantasy knickknack. How about a Cinderella coach teapot or cookie jar?

1257. Get a huge box, punch some air holes in it, get inside, have a friend gift-wrap it leaving the air holes uncovered, and have it delivered to your mate.

1258. Plan to have a memory night when the two of you must bring five happy memories on note cards to share.

1259. Send a cookie bouquet instead of flowers.

1260. Serve oysters and champagne and see what happens!

1261. Spend a night in a castle or mansion. Remember that atmosphere is important to romance.

1262. Create a romantic bubblebath by adding red food coloring to the bath water.

1263. Create a mini–herb garden for your gourmet cook on her kitchen window ledge.

1264. Make her feel like a topnotch model. Send her to a glamorous photography studio and have them work their magic.

1265. Surprise her with a diamond solitaire whose carat weight matches the number of years that you have been together or the number of decades that you have been together.

1266. Be a good sport and take her to her family reunion and turn it into a romantic mini-vacation.

1267. Read the story of Romeo and Juliet to each other.

1268. On a special evening, dress in romantic vintage clothing.

1269. Pick out wedding gifts for friends together. Always get into that romantic frame of mind, any way that you can.

1270. Dance the "Anniversary Waltz" only with your lover.

1271. Open a Visa or Mastercard account for your love with a huge credit balance before her next shopping expedition.

1272. Always help each other get through life's up and downs, but try to add as many romantic touches as you can.

1273. If your mate is trying to stop smoking and is using patches, cut them into little heart shapes.

1274. Check out the latest books on birth order to learn how it can affect a couple's relationship.

1275. Treat your love to a new, beautiful smile: Give your love braces.

1276. Tell her she is smart.

1277. Tell her she is sexy.

1278. Give her a classic gift, but with a twist: pearls with a difference.

    Black pearls   Seed pearls
    Freshwater pearls

Ask your jeweler to see a selection.

1279. Treat her to a kissing wardrobe—a new tube of lipstick for each day of the week.

1280. Don't consider breaking up as a passport to freedom. Think of it as a huge mistake.

1281. Make love from sunset to sunrise.

1282. Make love from sunrise to sunset.

1283. Studies confirm that couples who are in good physical condition enjoy sex more than those who aren't in good shape.

1284. Have a steady circle of close "couple" friends.

1285. Consult your mate before making plans to go out alone with your own circle of friends.

1286. Never insist on being socially active, as a couple, with someone your partner doesn't like.

1287. Keep in mind that a passionate kiss burns over twenty calories. What a great way to lose weight!

1288. After a party, enjoy your couple time of sharing "party gossip."

1289. Pursue activities that will enable you to meet other couples that share similar interests.

1290. Create your own private signal to alert your love when you are ready to leave a party.

1291. Know that a fabulous sex life requires lots of emotional foreplay.

1292. Sex is not about performance, so get that silly notion out of your head.

1293. Secrets of staying in love:
Flexibility   Fun
Forgiveness

1294. Long-term lovers agree: lovemaking improves with time.

1295. Give feedback to your lover on ways to improve your sex life.

1296. Do a remake of the society page of your Sunday newspapers: Cut out a couple of photos and replace them with photos of the two of you. Add some fun captions, and wait for your mate's reaction as he skims through the paper.

1297. Camp out in a sleeping bag made for two.

1298. Tuck romantic bookmarks into the books your love is currently reading.

1299. During the Christmas holidays, turn off all the lights in the house except for the Christmas tree and dream together by the glow of the tree.

1300. Create a "couple's binge day" when you eat too many chocolates, send too many flowers, and love each other even more than usual.

It is better to understand a little
than to misunderstand a lot.
— ANATOLE FRANCE

1301. Help each other maintain a strong sense of values.

1302. Give a gift to your lover on St. Patrick's Day for a nice little surprise. After all, most people don't give a present on this holiday, so your gift will be doubly appreciated. We suggest:
Irish love poems
A green after-dinner drink, crème de menthe
Green nighties
Green silk boxers
Green silk tie or scarf
Shamrock chocolates

1303. Be nice to strangers just because you are in love and feeling wonderful. Besides, your kindness will come back to you both and make your relationship even better.

1304. Give her a Waterford ring holder for her engagement ring when it isn't on her finger.

1305. Thank your lover, and praise your lover, when she does romantic gestures for you.

1306. Talk. Communicate. Converse with each other regularly. Questions to open up romantic dialogues:
What is your favorite romantic date?
What is your most romantic memory?
When did you fall in love?
What gestures touch your heart the most deeply?
When do you like to make love?

1307. Romantic rule: The more romantic gestures you make, the easier it will be for you to become a romantic person.

1308. It is especially important for husbands whose wives are pregnant to do extra-romantic gestures for her to keep their romance alive.

1309. Even on tiny anniversaries, use anniversary theme napkins for cocktails and also at dinner.

1310. Take a mini-mini-vacation. Take the afternoon off and go to a nearby town and have a grand time together.

1311. If you are going through a hard time in your relationship, do what the experts recommend. Fake it till you make it!

1312. Present her with a beautiful English tea set like those available from Cash's of Ireland.

1313. Replace all of his poker chips with heart-shaped ones before his next night out with the boys.

1314. Most people spend a minimum of twelve years in school learning skills to enable themselves to get a job. Yet, most people don't spend any time learning about relationships. You need to learn how to create a healthy, loving relationship. So study romance!

1315. On cold nights, warm your hands under hot, running water before you touch your lover.

1316. Sit down to meals together instead of rushing through them on your way to other activities.

1317. Purchase a wonderful picnic basket and blanket. Make plans to put them to use for at least six romantic picnics a year.

1318. Take her on a dream fashion vacation. She doesn't pack any clothes, but buys all new ones once you get to your destination.

1319. For your walking and singing in the rain, have matching raincoats and umbrellas.

1320. Plan a romantic, good-natured prank to pull on your mate on April Fool's Day.

1321. Run your fingers through your lover's hair.

1322. Buy a hammock for two for lazy summer afternoons together.

1323. Go materialistic and give her *all* the tangible desires of her heart.

1324. Host a cookout for two. He can do the grilling, and you can fix the potatoes and salads. Fix dessert together.

1325. Create your own secret garden for two.

1326. Make a giant heart out of freshly fallen snow in her front yard. Color it red with food coloring and attach a little love note.

1327. Give your love a three-dimensional puzzle of a cupid or heart.

1328. Browse a farmer's market for fresh and different little gifts for your lover.

1329. Purchase a set of matching luggage to announce to the traveling world that you are a couple.

1330. Place a dough heart on your pumpkin pie for Thanksgiving dinner. After all, isn't your mate one of your greatest blessings?

1331. Because she is your earthly angel, give her an angel gift:
An ornament   A figurine
A book on angels

1332. Start a romantic book club where you and your love can lead the discussions.

1333. Spread a lovely quilt on the ground and spend the evening stargazing.

1334. Hang a heart or cupid flag outside on your anniversaries.

1335. Attend a theater production of *Romeo and Juliet*.

1336. Kiss her hand when you part company.

1337. Check out your local radio stations to find one that plays only love songs.

1338. When she is in the hospital, send her a balloon bouquet on each day she is there.

1339. When you are both leaving the house, help her put her coat on.

1340. When you are dining out, let her order first.

1341. Place heart-shaped confetti in her briefcase when she is working really long hours, to remind her of your love.

1342. Hire a limousine to take the two of you to all your favorite spots that hold special meaning in your relationship.

1343. Use red dishes to create some very romantic table settings.

1344. When your love is a little short of cash, present him with a bouquet or wreath made out of money.

1345. Read between the lines. Hey, it makes for some very interesting, romantic moments.

1346. Create some gift excitement by giving your most expensive gift as the last present. Let each gift that you present be more valuable than the previous one.

1347. Have a romantic bumper sticker made for his car at a print shop.

1348. When he takes an extended business trip, pack a pen, stationery, and stamps in his suitcase so that he can *easily* keep in touch with you.

1349. Get an audiotape of Leo Buscaglia reading his books, to learn about love.

1350. Give her an outfit like one her favorite model wears when she goes out on the town.

1351. Hang matching Christmas stockings on the mantel for Santa to fill with romantic gifts.

1352. Get two kittens and name them after a famous couple.

1353. Take her to the whimsical Mary Engelbreit store in St. Louis. We guarantee that she will find tons of wonderful cards and gifts that speak to her heart.

1354. When your lover gives you a compliment, accept it graciously.

1355. Wear your mate's favorite fragrance on big dates.

1356. Make friends with your lover's:
Family　　　　　　　Friends
Coworkers　　　　　Animals

1357. Keep in mind that learning to love well is a never-ending lesson in life.

1358. The only romantic gift that you can't give is trust. It must be earned!

1359. Always cuddle after sex.

1360. Become a one-person support group for your mate during hard times.

1361. Romantic rule: Courtship should not cease when you say, "I do."

1362. Stop thinking of your lover as a home improvement project. Accept him as he is.

1363. Realize that if you put your relationship on auto-pilot, it will probably go off course.

1364. We hope you know that the more often you mention breaking up as a solution to your problems, the more likely it is to occur.

1365. Modern anniversary gifts:
First—clocks
Fifth—silverware
Tenth—diamond jewelry
Fifteenth—watches
Twentieth—platinum
Twenty-fifth—silver
Fiftieth—gold

1366. Stop correcting your mate's irrelevant mistakes.

1367. Ways that romance has changed through the years:
Women are more assertive than ever before
Dating is more relaxed
Monogamy is back in style
Couples are more interested in romance

1368. When you spend the night at a friend's home and you are given a room with twin beds, push them together for a night of cuddling.

1369. Get matching silk pajamas or share a set of his. She gets the top and he gets the bottoms.

To thine own self be true, and it must follow as the night the day, thou canst not then be false to any man.
— WILLIAM SHAKESPEARE

1370. Give her complete control of the electric blanket. You know, it is the little things that mean a lot.

1371. Fold the dinner napkins into heart shapes for your next romantic dinner for two.

1372. Give him a fabulous humidor to keep his cigars nice and fresh. To make it a romantic present, fill it with chocolate cigars and rose petals when it is first given to your love.

1373. Reasons to consider marriage:
You are in love
You know that your love is the one
You want to have a family together and you love each other

1374. While you are on vacation, hang a new robe and gown in the bathroom for her to find when she steps out of the shower.

1375. Appreciate having someone to come home to in the evenings. Remember, a lot of people don't have someone special in their lives.

1376. When you send mail to your lover, address it to his nickname instead of his formal name.

1377. When you pray together, thank God for your relationship.

1378. Prepare a compliment jar. Take strips of paper and write sincere compliments on each one. Place all the papers in a pretty glass jar and give it to your love during a hard time in his life.

1379. Eliminate all unnecessary criticisms about your mate. Trust us, most are not necessary and they certainly are romance killers.

1380. Keep in mind that a lack of effort and commitment in your relationship is a decision to be unhappy.

1381. Traditional anniversary gifts:
    First—paper
    Fifth—wood
    Tenth—tin
    Fifteenth—crystal
    Twentieth—china
    Twenty-fifth—silver
    Fortieth—ruby
    Fiftieth—gold

1382. Cut household items into heart shapes. Use simple things like sponges, napkins, and paper plates.

1383. When his camera has film in it, secretly take a picture of yourself holding a sign that expresses your love for him.

1384. Ask your mail carrier for the newest stamps that look romantic.

1385. Hide a zillion pencils in her office desk that are covered in hearts and other romantic motifs.

1386. Order some personalized rubber stamps that suit your own romantic nature to use for love letters or on white paper as gift wrap decorations.

1387. For a mate who loves to spend time in her garden, give a set of garden steps or stepping stones that have romantic sayings on them.

1388. Give a fun little leather-and-lace gift, like:
    Lace gloves and a leather handbag
    Lace socks and leather shoes

1389. While she is on an extended business trip, move her to her dream home and give her the thrill of a lifetime.

1390. For one month, give up placing demands on each other.

1391. Overwhelm her by giving a gift certificate from every:
Lingerie shop in town
Dress shop in town
Jewelry store in town
If you live in a large city, give gift certificates from shops in a certain area of your city.

1392. Place an elegant chaise longue in her bedroom to add a touch of glamour.

1393. Install a ceiling fan in your bedroom for those hot summer nights.

1394. Give your lover an interest-free loan (but ask for the interest back in hugs and kisses).

1395. Decorate his office for him in a rich style.

1396. Give him a "manly" new vehicle like a:
Truck   Moped
Snowmobile   Jeep
Motorcycle

1397. For your anniversary, get a classic car from the year that you met or were married.

1398. Work some overtime to make extra money to be able to afford a dream trip for the two of you.

1399. Get a part-time job to earn extra money so that you can buy your lover a dream present.

1400. Place Valentine decorations throughout your home a week before the big day.

1401. Put red or pink Christmas lights on plants and trees to decorate for Valentine's Day.

1402. Bake heart-shaped cookies and cakes throughout the year.

1403. In the fall, take a covered bridge tour together.

1404. Leave a trail of rose petals for her to find you.

1405. Win a prize for her at a local carnival or amusement park.

1406. When she gets a promotion, buy her a new desk set for her fabulous new office.

1407. When your significant other moves to a new apartment, give a romantic housewarming gift such as a:
Bottle of fine wine
Bottle of champagne
Painting of a beautiful garden scene
Framed photograph of the two of you
Heart-shaped rug

1408. Send a Waterford perfume bottle to her at the office so that she'll be the center of attention as she tells everyone just how terrific you are.

1409. Throw a romance party. Invite your friends and serve wine and heart-shaped appetizers. Ask everyone to bring an exchange gift that has a romantic theme. Be creative.

1410. Hold her gently in your arms and rock her to sleep.

1411. Stay awake all night together.

1412. Make a dream come true for your love by:
Giving her tickets to a sold-out show
Introducing him to a sports hero
Proposing marriage

1413. When he wants to wear a team shirt, present him with the whole ball of wax:

Team jacket	Team sweatshirt
Team jersey	Team baseball cap

1414. Take a trip outside the continental United States for a touch of glamour and romance.

1415. Take a long trip aboard the Love Boat.

1416. Celebrate at least one holiday a month together.

1417. Write a check to your mate for a million:

Kisses	Hugs
Back rubs	Love letters

1418. Make a surprise deposit in her checking account before she goes shopping with her friends.

1419. Show you care by being *extra* nice to her:

Friends	Family
Boss	Coworkers

1420. Throw a party for her and all her closest friends at a nearby spa and pamper the entire group.

1421. Get postcards of all the places you want to visit together and start sending them to him. To obtain the cards, contact:
Tourism Bureaus   Museum gift shops
Travel agents

A kiss that speaks volumes is seldom a first edition.
— OHIO STATE SUN DIAL

1422. Share an intimate secret with your lover.

1423. Play together:
Frolic in the swimming pool
Jog hand-in-hand
Dig out your old board games
Visit an arcade
Just have fun together

1424. Once a month, try to gain a new insight about your relationship.

1425. Call her your lover, as it sounds so romantic.

1426. Always be on time. That way you show respect for each other and you get to spend more time together.

1427. Too tired to cook a romantic dinner? Pick up some junk food on your way home and spend the evening just relaxing together in front of the fireplace.

1428. Create some gift excitement by giving little hints about your gift for your mate.

1429. Give up television viewing for a month and spend that time together doing fun activities instead of being couch potatoes.

1430. When you are extremely busy with work, meet for lunch instead of a dinner date. It beats not getting together at all.

1431. Start an add-a-bead, add-a-pearl, or charm bracelet for her. That way she will know that you are planning future romantic gifts.

1432. Give him a gift certificate for lawn care service to free up his weekends so that he can spend more time with you.

1433. Treat your mate better than you treat your closest friends or beloved pet.

1434. Visit a trophy shop and create a trophy for your mate. Consider:
     World's best kisser
     Number one mate
     First place for great date
     Happiest time of my life

1435. When you give a present, think long and hard about what your mate would like to have. Consider his tastes, not just your preferences. This tip is especially important if you and your mate do not have the same tastes.

1436. Give a beautiful music box for an anniversary gift. How about one that plays "your song" or the "Anniversary Waltz."

1437. When shopping for a spectacular gift, you might well be on the way to making a fabulous selection if the gift seems too:
     Expensive   Impractical
     Extravagant   Outrageous

1438. Nurture your mate. Everyone needs some TLC.

1439. Go that extra mile for your love. Give that extra inch.

1440. Spend a few minutes each day:
     Showing your romantic feelings
     Expressing your feelings
     Planning upcoming dates
     Planning celebrations
     Thinking romantic thoughts
     Looking on the bright side of your relationship

1441. Look at your mate through rose-colored glasses.

1442. Law of relationships: Little kindnesses and remembrances greatly improve the quality of one's love life.

1443. Wear a T-shirt that expresses your love for your mate.

1444. If you have a habit of forgetting dates, anniversaries, and the like, get a calendar just to take care of relationship information.

1445. Tell her that you thought about her while you were at work. Let her know that she is very important in your life.

1446. Every time that you travel on an extended business trip, bring back a lovely gift for your mate that shows you put time, thought, and effort into buying it.

1447. Start collecting wedding vows that you like and use them to create your own unique ceremony.

1448. Write down what you did on all your dates together for an entire year. Read it on New Year's Eve to bring back some wonderful memories.

1449. Create a full life for yourself so that your romantic relationship is the icing on the cake of your life, and not the cake itself.

1450. Take charge of your love life. Create romantic moments instead of just waiting for them to happen.

1451. Know that the most important elements of romance can't be bought with money. Those important elements are:
Time   Appreciation
Affection

1452. Spend a rainy Saturday afternoon together creating a photo album out of all the photographs of the two of you.

1453. Find an autographed copy of her favorite romance novel to give as a remembrance of a special time.

1454. Plan a fantasy trip on the Orient Express or the *QE2*.

1455. Change your clothes to change your mood. In other words, if you want to feel romantic, dress in a romantic style of clothing.

1456. Start an appreciation campaign. Mail a list of reasons that your love should be thrilled to have you as the love of her life.

1457. Keep track of how much time you actually spend being romantic for one month. How would you rate yourself on the romance scale?

1458. Give him a bottle of "love medicine"—a tiny jar of red hots.

1459. Have an attitude of gratitude for the special relationship you two have been given.

1460. Send a beautiful bouquet of daffodils and tulips on the first day of spring or for the Easter holiday.

1461. Value your partner's feelings even when they differ from your own.

1462. Have a specific time during the workday when both of you say a silent prayer for your relationship.

1463. The most romantic places in the United States:

New Orleans	Hawaii
San Francisco	Niagara Falls
Lake Tahoe	Hilton Head, SC

1464. Create a home filled with love and laughter.

1465. When going out for a night on the town with your friends and not your lover, give her a long, passionate kiss good-bye.

1466. Do something romantic today, even if it is just finishing this book.

1467. Find out what it takes for your mate to be fulfilled and happy in your relationship.

1468. To put some magic in your relationship, take your love to see a magician's performance.

1469. Take it one day at a time when you are first starting to be romantic. If you try too much, you will burn out and we sure don't want that to happen!

1470. Watch reruns of romantic comedies together:
   I Love Lucy
   The Dick Van Dyke Show
   Mad About You

1471. Give a box of white chocolates to symbolize the purity of your love.

1472. Give it all that you've got by setting the scene for romance in a big way. Go to the most romantic setting that you can find, at the most romantic time of the year, at the most romantic time of night, and declare your love.

Life has no job nobler than that of love.
— AUTHOR UNKNOWN

1473. Become a romance detective to uncover:
  Your mate's likes and dislikes
  Current trends in dating
  Great romantic nightspots
  Stores that stock romantic gifts

1474. Be sure to touch base with each other throughout the day.

1475. Look for ways that make both of you feel connected to each other.

1476. Relax with your lover and stop trying to be the perfect mate.

1477. Keep in mind that intimacy can take place only when you are able to understand and accept your partner for who he really is.

1478. If you find that your marriage is lacking passion, consider:
  Taking a mini-vacation
  Pretending that you aren't married and are having an affair with one another
  Working hard at becoming more romantic

1479. Know that self-confidence will make up for any lack of physical beauty.

1480. Kissing is one of the most intimate bonds that two lovers can share, so try to be a great kisser. Why not read one of the newest books on the subject? You might just learn a lot!

1481. Remember that sexual contact shouldn't constitute all of your affectionate gestures.

1482. If you are uncomfortable talking about intimate subjects, please note that it gets easier the more you do it.

1483. For women only: Men appreciate intimacy and relationship more as they age. Just imagine what he will be like in ten years!

1484. Sometimes, a lot of preparation is required for great "spontaneous" sex.

1485. Sing "your song" everywhere you go. Get into a romantic mood.

1486. Make the most of springtime, when the whole world falls in love.

1487. Springtime in Paris—need we say more?

1488. Visualize your ideal romantic day before hopping out of bed in the morning.

1489. While you are out of town, give her some of your shirts to sleep in to remind her of you.

1490. Before you go on a trip together, get:
Special evening clothes
Great lingerie
Gifts to take along on the trip

1491. Place a Valentine's Day classified ad that tells just how very much you care.

1492. Place a big cupid on your front door and have red arrows leading your mate to find either you or a gift.

1493. Before the two of you head to a romantic ski resort, buy matching goggles and outfits.

1494. Always say, "Bless you" when your mate sneezes.

1495. Stay up with your mate when he has insomnia.

1496. Arrange things so that both of you can be members of the wedding party when your friends get married. Weddings are so romantic.

1497. Keep a piece of your wedding cake in your freezer forever!

1498. If you can't afford some of the more expensive romantic gifts or gestures, learn to work with the ones you have. Don't wait to get started!

1499. Host a lovely champagne brunch for your lover on the weekend.

Love is not blind—it sees more, not less.
But because it sees more, it is willing to see less.
— RABBI JULIUS GORDON

1500. Three of the worst romance killers:
Resentments   Grudges
Jealousy

1501. Copy the romantic gestures of happy couples. Add your personal touches.

1502. Put love notes in plastic Easter eggs and hide them for your lover to find on Easter morning.

1503. Buy a new set of designer sheets for a touch of sophistication in your bedroom.

1504. Occasions to give a stuffed animal:
Teddy bear—no occasion needed
Easter bunny—for Easter
Anniversaries—little ones, that is!
When your love is sick
When your mate needs a little bit of cheering up

1505. Instead of watching the ball game, tape it, take her out, and watch the game after she goes to bed.

1506. Talk a little "babytalk" to your lover if you get the vibes to do so.

1507. Secretly check his schedule to plan a great time to kidnap him from the office.

1508. Plan a beautiful beach wedding in Hawaii.

1509. Use a soft, special tone of voice when you speak to your lover about your love.

1510. Give him an ice bucket filled with a bottle of good champagne and two crystal flutes.

1511. Get together on a very foggy night and pretend that you are in London.

1512. Resolve old grievances—NOW!

1513. Your music library should include these romantic styles of music:

Vocal	Instrumental
Classical	Adult contemporary

1514. Send anniversary cards on the date of your wedding each month for the entire year.

1515. Give her a diamond anniversary ring that will let her know that you really would marry her all over again.

1516. If she has a favorite work of art and you are unable to buy the original, give her a good copy of it.

1517. When your sister gets married, be sure that your love gets asked to be a bridesmaid.

1518. Explore your spirituality together—it will deepen your relationship.

1519. Carry in the heavy bags of groceries for her and slip a tiny note in the bottom of a bag for her to find when she unpacks them.

1520. Order for her at restaurants that you have been to but she hasn't.

1521. For a special breakfast, fix heart-shaped:

Eggs	Waffles
Pancakes	Toast
Fruit cutouts	

1522. Make great music together at home by using a karaoke machine and taping your duet.

1523. Prepare a program that lists all the planned events for your very special night out on the town and give it to your lover the day before the big event to create a bit of added excitement about the date.

1524. Go to your library and get some travel guides that are just for couples and get started planning your getaway.

1525. Keep your relationship on the cutting edge by staying up to date on the latest:

Trends	Products
Styles	Events

1526. Keep in mind that picturesque settings often lead to romantic feelings.

1527. Host a little backyard luau and dress in Hawaiian-style clothing.

1528. Help your mate obtain:

Dreams	Goals
Success	Recognition
Unique forms of self-expression	

1529. Get your wife and daughter matching mother/daughter outfits.

1530. If it is too early in the day to toast each other with champagne, toast each other with sparkling water.

1531. Dangerous romance killers:

Arrogance	Conceit
Selfishness	Egotism

1532. You should constantly be on the lookout for keepsakes, tokens of love, and souvenirs to buy for your significant other.

1533. Always show your lover:

Goodwill	Kindness
Tenderness	

1534. Give him a model of his dream car with a little note that says, "Someday."

1535. Give her a model of her dream house with a note that says, "Someday."

1536. Follow in Eve's footsteps, but with a twist; tempt him with a chocolate apple.

1537. Research her family tree and be sure to place your name beside hers.

1538. Take a horseback ride along a beautiful beach together at sunset.

1539. Dance the most romantic of dances, the tango.

1540. Ask a street musician to play "your song."

1541. Talk on the telephone for hours when you can't be together.

1542. Learn the latest dance steps together.

1543. Start a joint savings account.

1544. Carry an umbrella that is made for two on stormy date nights.

1545. Share a rich milkshake at an old-time diner.

1546. Arrange for a high school band to play "your song" at a local parade. Most band directors will be happy to help out your romantic schemes if you make a nice donation to their band funds.

1547. Create your own "Mirth Days."

1548. Get her a new exercise outfit for her aerobics class in a pretty shade of pink or red or with hearts on it.

1549. If your mate has a high-stress career, take him out to the country for a weekend of R and R (romance and relaxation).

1550. Give a gift of a wake-up service to a mate who can't get out of bed in the mornings.

1551. If she mentions that she would love to have a certain style of dress but can't find it, hire a dressmaker to create it for her.

1552. Rent a huge banquet hall and throw a huge party in his honor for no special occasion.

1553. Stroll through an arts and crafts show to look for unique gifts for your mate.

1554. Have elegant engraved invitations made for her surprise party and save one for her scrapbook.

1555. Get a car alarm for his new car. Have it secretly installed and leave a little note telling him that you just wanted to look after his "new love."

1556. If you want to give her a ruby ring or bracelet but find that it is too expensive, give the other popular red stone that costs much less. Give her a garnet.

1557. Present her with a home safe to store her jewelry in and have a lovely piece of jewelry tucked inside for her to find.

The one word above all others that makes marriage successful is "ours."
— ROBERT QUILLEN

1558. Know that sometimes the best friends that the two of you can have are the friends that you make together.

1559. Keep in mind that your mate doesn't have to love all your friends. Give each other room to have personal friends within the relationship.

1560. Just because the two of you are a couple, don't exclude singles from your social circle. You two need friends of all lifestyles to keep your relationship vital and alive.

1561. When she is in a bad mood, give her some bright wardrobe accents to brighten her spirits.

1562. Give her a new love seat for her living room.

1563. Take her to the important fashion shows in:
    New York   London
    Paris
    Be sure to buy her a new frock or two!

1564. Treat your mate to some status symbols for a touch of glamour.

1565. Slip a sterling silver compact into her cosmetic bag.

1566. Send chocolate truffles instead of a traditional box of chocolates.

1567. Buy a gorgeous crystal chandelier to hang in your bedroom.

1568. Keep a brainstorming list of ways to please your mate. Add to it often and then do the items from it on a regular basis.

1569. Get her favorite celebrity to propose for you.

1570. If you have messed up, send a "forgive me" bouquet after you make up in person.

1571. Give her a gold key to symbolize that she has the key to your heart.

1572. Know that a healthy romance improves one's self-esteem. It doesn't take away from one's self-image.

1573. Reasons to send flowers:
    First date anniversary
    First kiss anniversary
    Your lover is sick
    Your lover got a promotion
    Your lover has a new home
    Wedding anniversary
    Engagement anniversary
    First night of your honeymoon
    Last night of your honeymoon
    After an argument
    Her dog is sick
    Day of a bridal party for the two of you
    Her best friend got married and she is single
    She had a major fight with a friend or her mom
    Your mate got a big promotion

1574. Keep in mind that the best reason to send flowers is for no special occasion at all!

1575. Even if you have been married for twenty years, be sure to continue to date each other.

1576. Feed your lover:
    Chocolates   Tropical fruits
    Gourmet finger foods

1577. Always go to the theater to see the latest romantic movies.

1578. Rent a great romantic movie for a quiet night at home. We suggest:
Sleepless in Seattle
The Mirror Has Two Faces
When Harry Met Sally
One Fine Day
The American President
Chapter Two

1579. Imagine that you will never see your lover again and then write a long love letter to her telling her what she has meant to you.

1580. Rules for choosing a great restaurant for a romantic evening. Look for one that:
Requires dressing up for dinner
Is elegant
Has candles and flowers on the tables
Has fabulous food (especially desserts)
Has a fireplace
Has dancing

1581. Know that extravagance goes a long, long way in the world of romance.

1582. Learn to speak the language of love—French.

1583. Keep in mind that chivalry is back in style.

1584. Dine by candlelight at least once a week. Even a frozen dinner will taste and look better!

1585. Don't just say you love your mate. Show him in zillions of ways that you love him.

1586. Rules for a night of great romance:
No children　　　　No interruptions
No telephones　　　No pets
No workplace chitchat

1587. Sometimes one of the best ways to be romantic is to do a simple gesture in a big way. For example, if he likes cigars, send him a year's supply of them.

1588. Look for romantic inspiration everywhere you go.

1589. To make your love feel important, give her your full attention.

1590. Always strive to be the most romantic person in the world! The dividends are priceless!

1591. Keep it in the back of your mind that men and women are equally romantic.

1592. If you want to choose a low-cost romantic restaurant, look for:
> Quaint neighborhood establishments
> Ethnic foods
> Dark decor
> Good reviews on the cuisine

1593. Never allow yourselves to get into a predictable rut where you just keep on doing the same old stuff. Stir things up!

1594. Find a way to share each other's interests and hobbies. Sometimes, a little interest can move a relationship a long, long way.

1595. Call your lover at the office to say:
> Hurry home   I miss you
> Meet me   I love you
> Thanks for last night

1596. Ask a radio disk jockey to dedicate a song to your love.

1597. Enter yourselves in a Valentine contest. Radio and television stations are notorious for these promotions during the month of February.

1598. Pack a gourmet picnic lunch and take it to her office for a midday touch of romance.

1599. Sing "your song" to her as she falls asleep in your arms tonight.

1600. Pray for your relationship.

1601. Whisper. Whisper. Whisper. Everything sounds sexier when whispered in a lover's ear.

1602. Spend a lazy summer afternoon in bed.

1603. Whisk him away on a surprise weekend getaway. You'll need:
Hotel accommodations
His schedule cleared
His suitcase packed
Money and credit cards
A sense of adventure

1604. The next time that you are going away on an extended business trip, give your lover a teddy bear or puppy to keep your mate company.

1605. Prepare your partner's favorite meal for him. Call his mother to get the recipe if you don't have it.

1606. Qualities for men to cultivate:
Chivalry   Gallantry
Good manners

1607. E-mail him an unexpected love note.

Love is like quicksilver in the hand.
Leave the fingers open and it stays in the palm;
clutch it and it darts away.
— DOROTHY PARKER

1608. Fax a love letter to your mate.

1609. Know your lover's sizes so that you can give the perfect-fitting gift.

1610. Keep a collection of tapes of romantic music in your car.

1611. Take off your eyeglasses when you kiss.

1612. When you send a greeting card, do it with a little panache:
Send more than one
Send a huge card
Send it by registered mail
Send it by a special messenger
Deliver it in person

1613. Bake a huge chocolate chip cookie and put a loving message on it with icing.

1614. Make a heart-shaped pizza and spell out "luv ya" in pepperoni.

1615. Give a romantic CD for a little anniversary gift. We suggest:

Yanni	Michael Bolton
Luther Vandross	Natalie Cole
Johnny Mathis	Barbra Streisand
Whitney Houston	

1616. Get out of your dating rut. Choose something that the two of you have never done together from *2002 Things to Do on a Date*. Make plans to do it this coming weekend.

1617. Savor the special moments instead of rushing through life.

1618. Give homemade gifts that speak from the heart.

1619. Meet her for lunch at the mall when she is out on a major day of shopping.

1620. Give her a gift certificate to her favorite store.

1621. Secretly slip a hundred-dollar bill in her wallet before she goes shopping.

1622. When you set a romantic table, use:

The good china	Sterling flatware
Cloth napkins	Candles
Tablecloth/placemats	A floral centerpiece

1623. Our picks for romantic foods and beverages:

Strawberries	Chocolates
Champagne	Wine
Caviar	Brandy
Lobster	Grapes

1624. Invest in romance:

Diamonds	Gold

1625. Shop for new romantic looks for your home together.

1626. Kiss goodnight.

1627. Compliment your mate in public. It doubles the benefits of the compliment.

1628. Kiss good-bye when parting.

1629. Send a formal invitation through the mail for your next date.

1630. Send chocolate roses instead of long-stemmed red ones.

1631. Give a prepaid telephone calling card to your mate the next time she leaves town so that she can call you free of charge.

1632. On your anniversary, go to a craft store and purchase a wedding cake topper and place it proudly on your dessert for a little touch of romance.

1633. Refer to your bedroom as the boudoir.

1634. Cut out cute romantic cartoons from the newspapers and send them to your mate.

1635. Ask your lover to give you a list of his ten top dream vacation spots. Call your travel agent and turn his dream into a reality.

1636. Have your mate give you a list of her dream gifts. Ask her to update it on a regular basis so that you will always have great ideas for presents.

1637. Send him to a baseball training camp for a week. Halfway through the trip, surprise him by meeting him there and turning the sports trip into a second honeymoon.

1638. Keep a little romantic gift tucked away just in case your romantic suitor gives you a gift and you want to reciprocate.

1639. When shopping for anniversary gifts, think:
Extra-special
Romantic
Unique to your partner's tastes
Nonpractical

1640. Make a list at the beginning of each month of romantic gestures and dates that you can do and vow to do them.

1641. Take her on the most popular date in the entire world—go out for dinner.

1642. If you want her to feel sexy, give her a gift certificate to Victoria's Secret.

1643. How to buy elegant gifts on a budget:
Shop sales
Shop in advance of the holiday rush
Always be on the lookout for great gifts
Shop outlets
Shop warehouse stores
Shop antiques stores
Browse flea markets

1644. Always keep a bottle of champagne on ice just for the little occasions that pop up and need to be celebrated in a special way.

1645. Want to give your love fabulous jewels, but your budget won't allow it? Try a little creative substitution:
Instead of cultured pearls, give seed pearls.
Instead of a diamond engagement ring, give a birthstone engagement ring.
Instead of a gold bracelet, give a sterling silver one.

1646. If she wants an engagement ring but you aren't ready to make that commitment yet, tell her before the next big holiday that a ring isn't coming as her gift, to save both of you from heartache.

1647. Remember that how you present a gift is almost as important as the gift itself.

1648. Send postcards to your love while you are away on a business trip.

1649. Have cute nicknames for each other. Don't use any sarcastic ones.

1650. Visit a honeymoon resort on your next vacation.

1651. Spend at least one night a year in the bridal suite of a lovely hotel.

1652. Take your lover along on your next business trip.

1653. Give her a set of love coupons, which are available at most bookstores and gift shops in early February. Buy a couple of sets and give them throughout the year. Or make your own love coupons.

1654. Call in advance for dates. Yes, you should ask even your marriage partner of fifty years for dates in advance!

1655. Put a great deal of effort into planning your vacations.

1656. Put a great deal of effort into planning your dates.

1657. Write a greeting on your love's morning newspaper.

1658. Look for romantic tips in popular:
Magazines   Movies
Newspapers   Television shows

A great lover is one who never loses his childlike heart.
— AUTHOR UNKNOWN

1659. Give her the gift of her favorite fragrance in all its forms:
Bath powder   Candles
Bath gels and oils   Lotions

1660. Carry a list of your partner's sizes in your wallet.

1661. Replace all of the game pieces of her favorite childhood boardgame with heart-shaped pieces in a variety of colors.

1662. Renew your wedding vows.

1663. Simply read over your wedding vows to refresh your memory about what you promised.

1664. Have Saturday night's dinner catered in your home and enjoy staying in together.

1665. Hire a band or pianist to play for you and your lover at your home.

1666. Fill her glove compartment with flowers.

1667. Let him know just how much you appreciate him. Men need to feel appreciated just as much as women do.

1668. Bake your lover a birthday cake.

1669. Get your mate a gorgeous birthday cake from the best bakery in town.

1670. Go on a camping trip and enjoy evenings under the stars together.

1671. Send your children to the baby-sitter's, grandmother's, or a friend's for the weekend.

1672. Create a sense of mystery and excitement when planning your next party.

1673. Prepare an elaborate scavenger hunt for his next birthday.

1674. Buy your lover a piece of antique jewelry that has a history or romance.

1675. Hide a gift of jewelry in:
An ice cube   A birthday cake

1676. Tuck a small fun gift into a box of Cracker Jack.

1677. Fill the medicine cabinet with heart confetti to start your lover's day off in a romantic way.

1678. Make up a crossword puzzle that highlights your history together.

1679. Create a collage of your relationship.

1680. Leave a set of clues to where your next date will be and then meet your love there to have an interesting beginning to a big date.

1681. Pick wildflowers for her while you are on a picnic.

1682. Give him tickets to a:
Sporting event   Rock concert
Jazz club   Fitness club

1683. Give her tickets to the:
Opera   Symphony
Ballet

1684. Make your lover a major priority in your busy life.

1685. Send your children over to a friend's house for the afternoon so that you and your spouse can have a little time for romance.

1686. Plant a surprise flower garden for her.

1687. Send flowers to your mate's mother on your mate's birthday.

1688. Give her a charm bracelet that consists of charms that hold special meaning for the two of you.

1689. Send your love flowers while you are out of town.

1690. Keep a picture of your mate on your desk at the office.

1691. Give her a sterling silver bud vase and promise always to keep a fresh rose in it.

1692. After the next big snowstorm, clean off his windshield in the shape of a heart.

1693. For women only: Seek gift-giving advice from:

His dad	His mom
His coworkers	His friends
His siblings	His boss

1694. For men only: Seek gift-giving advice from:

Her best friend	Her mom
Her coworkers	Her sisters
A professional shopper	

1695. Get to know your local florist and ask his help in picking out unique floral arrangements.

A man should keep his friendships in constant repair.
— SAMUEL JOHNSON

1696. While away from your mate, send a bouquet of forget-me-nots.

1697. Buy a "You are special today" plate and use it for your mate's birthdays and your anniversaries.

1698. Visit your local nursery and buy a rose bush that carries her name.

1699. Send your love a box of divinity with a note saying that you think she is heavenly.

1700. Learn to play "your song" on the piano.

1701. Gently wake him with kisses when he snores and keeps you awake.

1702. Send her gourmet lunches every Friday for a year. It is guaranteed to start the weekend off on the right foot.

1703. Pretend that you and your mate won't see each other after tonight. See what happens!

1704. Wrap all his birthday presents in a different birthday paper to make the gifts look even more special.

1705. Pretend to be:
Scarlet and Rhett   Tarzan and Jane
Romeo and Juliet

1706. On momentous birthdays, find greeting cards that acknowledge the years.

1707. Pretend to be chained together at the ankles for a Saturday.

1708. It is very hard to beat a gift of homemade fudge, cookies, or brownies when you want to treat your love. Start your ovens!

1709. Prepare a fabulous Easter basket for your mate. Be sure to include all her childhood favorites.

1710. Read *In Style* magazine to get ideas on fashionable and trendy ways to show you care.

1711. Every time that you pass a candy store, treat your mate to a small box of candy.

1712. Give him a new tie to wear for his next big meeting at work.

1713. Serve breakfast by candlelight.

1714. Treat her to a lovely peignoir set.

1715. Hire a limousine to bring her home from the office on your anniversary or her birthday.

1716. Keep a diary of your favorite moments together from your lover's birthday to her next birthday. Give it to her for her birthday.

1717. Sign a romantic card "Your secret love" just to spice things up a bit.

1718. Break out the fabulous bottle of wine that you have been saving for a special occasion and turn tonight into a special evening for two.

1719. Take a no-cost vacation for two. Stay at a friend's vacation home or visit your parents.

1720. Show up on his commuter ride home from the office with a romantic letter and candy.

1721. Check out the low weekend rate offered at most major hotel chains when planning a getaway. Ask for special honeymoon offers, too.

1722. Read the reviews of new restaurants, plays, and shows to look for exciting date ideas.

1723. Smile warmly at your lover.

1724. Start a romance fund. Save for a fabulous honeymoon, second honeymoon, or vacation getaway.

1725. Buy an RV and turn it into your love nest on wheels.

1726. Start little holiday traditions:
> Preparing holiday meals together
> Fixing a Christmas stocking for each other
> Trimming a tree together
> Carving a pumpkin for Halloween together
> Decorating Easter eggs together
> Having your own fireworks on July 4th

1727. Walk down the street arm-in-arm.

1728. Spend the night at a romantic ski resort.

1729. Learn to communicate well with your mate.

1730. Take a massage class. Learn this art of relaxation. Consider taking this class together.

1731. Use a love poem as a bookmark.

1732. Stop by the nearest gift shop and purchase lots of wonderfully scented candles to light up your love life.

1733. Tape inspirational relationship messages on your bathroom mirror.

1734. Fall asleep in each other's arms.

1735. "Toe snuggle" under the covers.

1736. Treat her to breakfast, lunch, and dinner in bed whenever she is sick.

1737. Add a touch of glamour to her flannel nightgown. Hang a feather boa next to it.

1738. Tell your love to reserve a specific date at a specific time, but don't say why. Then surprise him with tickets to a fabulous sold-out show.

1739. Spoil him by doing all his least favorite chores for him.

1740. On birthday and anniversary cakes, use sparklers instead of candles.

1741. Give her some gifts to make her feel glamorous:
    Gift certificate to a spa
    Beauty treatments
    Designer clothes
    Gorgeous silk lingerie

1742. Instead of sending a birthday card, send a:
    Birthday poem
    Singing telegram
    Cake delivered by messenger
    Musical card

1743. Be sure that you celebrate both your engagement and wedding anniversaries.

1744. Stop by the liquor store and pick up a bottle of fine brandy to sip in front of the fire.

1745. On your mate's birthday, give a scrapbook of all your shared birthday celebrations. It will bring back some wonderful memories.

1746. On your anniversary, send her one bouquet for each year that you have been married.

1747. Want to make Mr. Hallmark happy? Send one romantic greeting card for each date that the two of you have shared.

1748. Bring home his favorite beverage and appetizer for a nice happy hour for two.

1749. Stop by the deli and pick up her favorite dessert for dinner tonight.

1750. Celebrate the first day of each new season by sending a seasonal bouquet.

The remembrance of the good done to those
we have loved is the only consolation
left us when we have lost them.
— DEMOUSTIER

1751. If you can't write poetry, borrow from the masters like Browning and Shakespeare.

1752. Always make an extra effort to be caring when your mate is sick:
Send flowers
Send a get well card
Prepare homemade soup
Bring magazines and books
Take him to the doctor

1753. Take a walk with your sweetheart in the first snowfall of the season.

1754. Make plans together for every major holiday.

1755. Create your own personalized greeting card. These are available at most large card shops.

1756. Plan a romantic trip to a honeymoon area like:
The Poconos   Niagara Falls
Great Smoky Mountains

1757. Send your love a romantic novel and make the most romantic part of the book your wildly romantic inscription.

1758. On a cold night, stay at home and snuggle under the covers.

1759. Unplug the television. See what happens!

1760. Give him a hand massage after he has been working hard with his hands.

1761. On an extremely cold morning, warm up her car for her before she leaves for the office.

1762. While your mate is in the shower, warm his towel in the dryer and hide a little love note inside the folded towel.

1763. Put confetti in greeting cards and also enclose some new pictures of the two of you.

1764. Create new lines to the old poem:
Roses are red,
Violets are blue,
Sugar is sweet
And so are you.
You don't even need to be a poet. Anyone can write a new line or two.

1765. Laugh together OFTEN.

1766. Send silly romantic jokes to each other just to brighten the day.

1767. Have your own couple's list of your favorite:

Restaurants	Songs
Activities	Beverages
Vacation spots	Artists
Shows	Recording artists
Movies	

1768. Give her a subscription to a bridal magazine just because she was once your bride.

1769. If you aren't ready to give her a diamond ring, how about giving a diamond of another style? We suggest:

Earrings	Pendant
Tennis bracelet	

1770. Surprise her by having dinner ready for her when she gets home tonight.

1771. Purchase all new ornaments for her Christmas tree. Select a romantic theme for the decorations.

1772. Recycle your love:
> Reread your old love letters from each other
> Re-create your first date
> Re-create your best date
> Reread your favorite love story

1773. To make a lovely picture of romance, frame:
> Your favorite romantic CD cover
> A love poem
> A love letter
> A photo of the two of you
> Your baby bracelets together
> Menus from romantic dinners you have shared
> Your wedding license
> Romantic cartoons
> Travel posters from your honeymoon

1774. Fall into a pile of fall leaves together.

1775. On New Year's Eve and your anniversary eve, make relationship resolutions together.

1776. Fix a memorabilia box of your relationship. Include:
> Photos   Ticket stubs
> Cards   Hotel room keys
> Dried flowers

1777. Hire a talented local artist to paint a romantic motto on your fireplace mantel. Our favorite: "Fairy tales do come true."

1778. Give her a small gift bag filled with seven kinds of bubble bath, one for every night of the week.

1779. Take him out to dinner at a wonderfully romantic French restaurant.

1780. Restaurant-hop for a little change. Pick the three most romantic restaurants that you know and have appetizers at one, dinner at another, and dessert at another.

1781. If you want a fabulous romantic setting to propose, take your love to one of the largest and loveliest mansions in the country that is open to the public, Viscaya, in Miami.

1782. Write a journal of the funny things that happen in your relationship and give it to your mate when he needs a little cheering up.

1783. *Forget* old arguments and hurts in addition to forgiving your mate.

1784. Get rid of all unromantic relationship habits, such as:
Yelling   Nagging
Name calling

1785. Discuss what a quality relationship means to both of you.

1786. If you have a routine dinner planned for tonight, spruce it up by changing the atmosphere to one of romance. Use:
Soft lighting   Mood music
Candles   Loving words

1787. Talk about your values, beliefs, ideas, and philosophies with each other.

1788. Plan big dates far, far in advance to give you both something to look forward to.

1789. Buy a lottery ticket together and agree to spend your winnings in only romantic ways.

1790. Shop together for clothing styles that are pleasing to both of you.

1791. Keep in mind that people on their deathbeds never wish that they had spent more time at the office, but many wish that they had spent more time with their loved ones.

1792. Take a class together one night a week:
Wine tasting   Gourmet cooking
Dog obedience   Creative writing

1793. Key phrases in romantic relationships:

"I am very sorry"	"I love you"
"Thank you"	"Please"
"Forgive me"	"I need you"
"I want you"	

1794. Kiss whenever you hear your secret code word. Yes, you need first to choose a romantic code word.

1795. Know that your lover is not a mind reader. Speak up and make your thoughts known.

1796. Make a toast to your lover at dinner tonight.

1797. Strike up your own conversation in your Internet chat room.

1798. Listen to your mate with your ears and your heart.

1799. Learn to read your mate's body language.

1800. Frame his childhood baseball mitt in a shadow box for his office.

1801. Attach a note to her car clock asking her to meet you at a specific time for a fabulous date.

1802. Trade romantic ideas with a trusted coworker.

Keep your eyes wide open before marriage,
and half-shut afterwards.
— BENJAMIN FRANKLIN

1803. Whenever you dine at a restaurant that has a little gift shop, pick up a little trinket such as a box of candy for your mate.

1804. Turn your grandmother's engagement ring into a drop pendant for her.

1805. Give her the most beautiful engagement ring you can afford. This is a ring that she will wear for the rest of her life, so spoil her a bit.

1806. Try to perform a new romantic gesture each week for a year. Are you feeling really romantic? Try a new gesture twice weekly.

1807. Sing "your song" in the shower as you get ready for a big night out.

1808. Give him a pair of stylish boxers.

1809. When he is out with the guys, arrange to have his favorite cocktail brought to him with your sentiments written on a napkin.

1810. Learn to use sign language so that you can send each other loving messages in a new way.

1811. Send your love a love letter from Santa Claus, Indiana, during the holidays. Contact the post office there for details.

1812. Give her a fabulous gift when she has a baby.

1813. If you have small children, always get her a Mother's Day gift from the children.

1814. If you have small children, always get him a Father's Day gift from the children.

1815. Decorate his office in a personal style by framing his:
Diplomas and certificates
Medals
Boy Scout badges
Baseball cards

1816. Play the game of Twister together.

1817. Give her a piece of gold jewelry for no special reason.

1818. When you can't kiss because one of you is sick, give each other chocolate kisses.

1819. If your mate isn't the romantic type, set an example for him through all your romantic gestures.

1820. Tell your mate that you want him to be romantic.

1821. Consider getting professional counseling to tweak your relationship.

1822. Always take advantage of a great dance band.

1823. Have a heart-to-heart talk with your lover.

1824. Buy his and her towels for your master bathroom.

1825. Be impetuous!

1826. Give your mate your wedding invitation framed in a lovely sterling silver frame.

1827. Frame your favorite playbills to hang on the wall in your den.

1828. Frame concert tickets that hold special memories for the two of you.

1829. Give her a lovely bride doll for an anniversary gift.

1830. Buy some stock in a diamond mine for him.

1831. Ingredients of a romantic dinner:

Cocktail	Appetizer
Fine wine	Gourmet food
Yummy dessert	After-dinner liqueur

1832. Turn your anniversary into a week-long celebration.

1833. Plan to take your love to a romantic community theater production.

1834. Take a trip to Quebec City, Canada, for the wintertime festivities.

1835. Give each other the freedom to be your true selves.

1836. Send her a *lifetime* subscription to her favorite magazine.

1837. Read the travel ads in bridal magazines to get ideas for a romantic getaway.

1838. Treat yourself to some fabulous French lingerie.

1839. Kiss the nape of your lover's neck.

1840. Leave a romantic, fun message at the hotel desk when he is out of town on a business trip.

1841. Listen to traditional wedding music.

1842. Make a cassette tape of all your favorite love songs.

1843. Wash your car before a big date.

1844. Hang a welcome home banner when he comes home from a trip.

1845. Each Christmas, go out and buy a special romantic ornament together.

The only gift is a portion of thyself.
— RALPH WALDO EMERSON

1846. Share a sleeping bag under the stars in your own backyard.

1847. Renew your vows in a flashy Las Vegas wedding chapel.

1848. Stroll along a deserted beach in the wintertime with your mate.

1849. Serve fruit, fine cheese, and champagne in bed tonight.

1850. After a bad day, cry on his shoulder.

1851. Browse through the travel section of a large city's newspaper and plan a quick trip together.

1852. Hold hands during dinner.

1853. Dine at quaint outdoor cafés when the weather permits.

1854. Choose spending time with her over spending time with the guys, and let her know of your choice.

1855. Give your mate your undivided attention.

1856. Stay up together to watch the last burning ember die out in the fire.

1857. Give him a jukebox filled with the songs that have special meaning for the two of you.

1858. Find a lovely pillow that has a romantic saying on it.

1859. Have a special bouquet of flowers waiting for her at your table when you arrive at the restaurant.

1860. Pretend that:
>Your television doesn't work
>Your phone cable has been cut
>Your lights work only on the dimmer switch
>You can't go outside because of bad weather

1861. When you dine out, ask for booths, corner tables, dark tables, or tables with a view, to make your evening out more romantic.

1862. On a cold evening, head over to a quaint coffeehouse and spend an hour talking over a steaming cup of java.

1863. The next time she has a big presentation at work, wait in her office to find out how she did on it.

1864. Give your love a copy of her favorite romantic movie on videotape.

1865. Take ballroom dance lessons together. Is there anything more romantic than a couple who can dance well together?

1866. Treat him to a big, comfortable easy chair to watch his ball games in on Saturday afternoons.

1867. Save your marriage—buy a dual-control electric blanket.

1868. Always date your love notes that you hide just in case they aren't found for a very long time.

1869. Give her an old-fashioned Raggedy Ann doll. It is the only doll that has a heart.

1870. Buy matching p.j.s and robes to lounge around in on the weekends.

1871. Never take your partner for granted.

1872. Read books about improving your sex life.

1873. Make yourself sexier:
>Lose five pounds   Exercise
>Get a new wardrobe   Try a new hairstyle
>Increase your self-esteem

1874. If you have had some problems in the past, agree to start the relationship over. A fresh start may be exactly what the two of you need to make a success of your relationship.

1875. Act silly together.

1876. Learn to let go of some of your inhibitions.

1877. Look at your life. Ask yourself if your love life gets enough of your attention.

1878. Make an adventure out of your next vacation. Go on a romantic African safari.

1879. Spend the next twenty-four hours in bed. Order out for food.

1880. Frame a favorite romantic movie poster for some inexpensive art.

1881. Buy a calendar for your mate and fill it with all kinds of dates for the two of you to share. You can mark it with just time for the two of you or specific dates, such as:

Dinners	Concerts
Movies	Ball games
Picnics	

1882. Frame your favorite quote about romance.

1883. Have a silk floral bouquet made to look like her bridal bouquet and have it placed in a lovely mahogany shadow box to give her for an anniversary gift.

1884. Write your own wedding vows.

1885. Take the television out of the bedroom.

1886. Host a picnic in your bedroom. Fill a basket with champagne, flowers, candy, gourmet foods, and soft music.

1887. Imagine wonderful things happening between the two of you.

1888. Get stuck in a revolving door together.

1889. Give him a tape of his favorite ball game for a thoughtful "little" anniversary gift.

1890. Hold hands during an airplane trip.

1891. Enjoy your shared history together. Isn't it nice to be with someone who knows all about you?

1892. Try to find a popular song that has your lover's name in it. Play it on your next date.

1893. Get a matchbook from his favorite restaurant and wrap it up with a note inviting him to dinner there.

1894. Meet for a middle-of-the-night meal.

1895. Learn the art of calligraphy so that you can make your love letters look wonderfully romantic.

1896. Frame the wedding vows from the ceremony when you renewed your vows.

1897. Have a poster-size enlargement made of your favorite photo of the two of you.

1898. Give her scented liners for her lingerie drawers.

1899. Have a fabulous piece of jewelry designed especially for her.

1900. Give him a gold watch for a milestone birthday or anniversary. Have it engraved with a romantic message on the back.

1901. "Tepee" his front yard and leave a romantic note. His neighbors will enjoy the show.

1902. Kidnap your lover away from the office for:
Lunch
An afternoon rendezvous
A getaway

1903. Let your love know your:
Fears   Hopes
Secrets

1904. Fill her shoes with gift certificates for pedicures.

1905. Name your puppy for your mate.

1906. Fill her handbag with new bills.

1907. Hang a streamer from the front porch declaring your love.

1908. On your lover's birthday, take her out for breakfast, lunch, and dinner.

1909. When she leaves the table at a restaurant to powder her nose, place a small but special gift at her place.

1910. Keep in mind that bridal magazines are a great source of ideas for romantic home decor and gift giving.

1911. Use pink light bulbs for romantic lighting.

1912. True romance = one love, one lifetime.

1913. Check with local inns, B&Bs, and hotels for their specials for nights out on the town.

1914. Run off together to live on a tropical island.

1915. Make every day a day to express your love.

1916. Great places to hide a gift so that your mate won't find it until the big celebration:
    Behind the refrigerator
    In the freezer in your garage
    In your toolshed or garage storage area
    In the guest bedroom closet
    In the bottom of the clothes hamper
    In the trunk of your car
    Behind seldom-read books on a bookshelf
    Taped to the back of a picture
    In the sleeve of a seldom-worn coat
    At your parents' home
    At your office
    At a friend's house
    At your neighbor's home

1917. Plan a scavenger hunt for your mate to find *you*.

1918. To get fresh ideas on romance, browse a bookstore in areas like:

Home decorating	Psychology
Relationships	Gift sections
Magazines	Foreign newspapers
Foreign magazines	

1919. Make up a romantic dart board and let your love take aim to win a gift or kiss.

1920. Be the one who does the most romantic gesture in your lover's life.

1921. Set up your own toll-free telephone number for your love to call you if she travels a lot.

1922. Hire a butler for her for a week, a month, or even a lifetime!

1923. Decorate her bicycle or car with hearts.

1924. Two characteristics of great partners:
Passionate   Compassionate

1925. For country-oriented lovers, give the romantic CD collection called *Real Luv*.

In love, as in politics, it is always a "third party"
that stirs up all the trouble—and throws
the machinery out of order.
— AUTHOR UNKNOWN

1926. Reasons to throw her a party:
Promotion at work
New hairstyle
Bad hair day
Her best friend got married and she is single
She is pregnant
You love her
It is her birthday

1927. Reasons to throw him a party:
He received a promotion
Bon voyage party before his big trip
A big game on television
He finished a project
It is his birthday
He got a dog
He is going to be a dad
He needs some cheering up

1928. Learn couples' ice skating or roller skating.

1929. Try giving unconditional love to your mate.

1930. Buy a bride-and-groom toasting set and make a very special toast to your love on your next anniversary.

1931. True romance is made up of:
Feelings   Gestures
Intimacies exchanged   Total commitment

1932. Stop eating out together at typical cookie-cutter chain restaurants. Start looking for romantic spots to dine at together.

1933. When you are away on business, call her every night at bedtime.

1934. Put your arm around her at the movies.

1935. Compliment her hairstyle every single time that she comes home from the salon.

1936. Hire a violinist to play during a romantic dinner.

1937. If you are a bad dancer, secretly sign up for dance lessons. Surprise your mate by taking her out for a fabulous night of dancing after you have completed the lessons.

1938. Give him a monogrammed silver case in which to carry his cigars.

1939. Learn how to quickly reconnect after being apart during the day.

1940. Avoid letting fear and embarrassment stop you from expressing your feelings and desires.

1941. Flirt with your mate even if you have been together for decades.

1942. If you need help with your sex life, send a SASE to the Association of Sex Educators, Counselors, Therapists, PO Box 238, Mt. Vernon, IA 52314 for a referral to a qualified therapist in your area.

1943. Get on the mailing lists of zillions of unique mail-order catalogs so that you can search out special gifts for your lover.

1944. Create four seasons of photographs of the two of you and change them with the arrival of each new season.

1945. Make love before bedtime.

1946. On your anniversary, recite the lyrics to "your song."

1947. Give her a list of the ten reasons that you love her more than any other person in the world.

1948. Write a five-page letter telling your love your recollections of your:

First meeting   First date
First kiss   The moment you fell in love

1949. Snuggle before going to sleep each night.

---

*Letters that should never have been written
and ought immediately to be destroyed
are the only ones worth keeping.*
— Sydney Tremayne

1950. Give up trying to change your mate. Instead, try improving yourself.

1951. Put your feelings on a theater marquee.

1952. Consider buying her a diamond in *each* of the most popular cuts:

Round   Pear
Emerald   Marquee

1953. Hire a skywriter to declare your love.

1954. Place your feelings up for the world to see on a rented billboard.

1955. Make a videotape of you declaring your love for your sweetheart.

1956. Know that there is no substitute for togetherness.

1957. Hide a diamond ring in the center of a rose bud. Use tweezers to insert it.

1958. During the commercials before a movie, place an ad declaring your love.

1959. Carve your initials on an old tree (be careful not to cut too deep or you will have the environmentalists after us).

1960. Fly a kite that tells her how you feel.

1961. Dance to swing music. It'll put you both in a fun, crazy, romantic mood.

1962. Save all the corks from the champagne bottles that you have shared with your love. Add ribbon and beads and string them together for a unique, romantic garland for your Christmas tree.

1963. Develop gift finesse. Buy clothing for your love that is:
In the correct size
From your love's favorite store
The correct color
A flattering style for your love

1964. If you mess up and forget a birthday or an anniversary, admit your mistake. Then make arrangements to celebrate the occasion in a manner that will be twice as nice as it would have been.

1965. Take your mate out for breakfast before work for a great romantic way to start the day.

1966. Make a list of five romantic restaurants that you and your lover haven't been to and vow to visit each one within the next few months.

1967. When you take your love out to dinner, have a gift waiting for her at the table.

1968. Get lost together on purpose for a little romantic adventure.

1969. Take a horse-drawn carriage ride at sunset.

1970. Search through your newspaper's classified ads for tickets to sold-out events.

1971. Never interrupt your phone calls with your lover to take other calls.

1972. Find out where she is staying on her business trip and have flowers waiting in her room.

1973. Ask your secretary, mom, friend, or coworker to remind you of all your important romantic anniversaries.

1974. Give your mate a gift certificate for lessons as an anniversary bonus gift. We suggest:

Golf	Tennis
Music	Swimming

These are all activities that you can enjoy together!

1975. Leave a trail of his favorite candy to lead him to a present or to you!

1976. Declare your feelings of love for your mate in a window display at a lovely store.

1977. At the beginning of each year, look through the new phone book for new restaurants that might be great romantic haunts for the two of you.

1978. Send your wife flowers on your children's birthdays.

1979. Great inexpensive "anniversary" gifts:

Love stories	Heart-shaped puzzles
Bottles of wine	Gourmet cookies
Movie tickets	CDs
Photo albums	Trinket boxes
Heart-shaped pillows	Lace
Perfume bottles	Plants
Flowers	T-shirts
Key chains	Ornaments
Self-help tapes	Candy
Videos	

1980. Ask your lover for a current picture to place on your nightstand.

1981. Gaze into each other's eyes.

1982. In the middle of a party, a movie, a dinner, or a chore, whisper something romantic to your lover.

1983. Stop by a Crabtree & Evelyn shop to pick up a sweet-smelling little gift for your love.

1984. Turn your bedroom into a romantic escape, not a TV and exercise equipment warehouse.

1985. Create a time capsule of your relationship. Bury it in your backyard or favorite park.

1986. Return to the basics of an old-fashioned romance:
Dignity   Manners
Courting   Rituals

1987. Eliminate any signs of competition between the two of you. You need to be a team.

1988. Read lots of books on social customs and entertaining to get new ideas for creating romance.

1989. Keep in mind that the old saying "Little things mean a lot" is especially true when it comes to romance.

1990. Pick out a constellation together and whenever you see it, think of your mate.

1991. Reasons to be romantic:
It will enhance your love life
It will bring you and your mate closer
It is fun and exciting
You will be the envy of other couples
Your sex life will improve
You will be happier in your relationship
Your chances of a breakup will drastically diminish
You will become a more passionate couple

1992. The most popular Valentine gifts:
Flowers   Candy
Lingerie   Perfume

1993. Ask yourself what changes you would make in your relationship if you had only one more year to live. Start making those changes.

1994. On a cold night when he is working late at the office, bring him a thermos of hot chocolate and some heart-shaped chocolate chip cookies.

1995. Choose a pendant or earrings that match the color of her eyes. For example:

Emeralds for green eyes
Sapphires for blue eyes
Tiger eyes for brown eyes

1996. Have a red anniversary:
Red roses
Bottle of red wine
Ruby ring
Red silk nightgown and robe
Ruby red slippers

1997. Restrain yourself from buying practical gifts unless they are requested. Even then, be sure to give a second little gift that means romance just to keep your relationship on the romance track.

1998. Name your yacht, car, or airplane for your lover.

1999. Send her a beautiful jewelry box filled with costume jewelry or, better yet, the real stuff!

2000. Celebrate February 29 in a way that she will remember for the next four years. Splurge! Plan! Get out of the box! Go romantically wild!

2001. Appreciate all the differences between men and women instead of complaining about them.

2002. Honor, cherish, love, respect, comfort, and keep your mate, and everything will fall into its romantic place.

The man and woman who can laugh at their love, who can kiss with smiles and embrace with chuckles, will outlast in mutual affection all the throat-lumpy, cow-eyed couples of their acquaintance. Nothing lives on so fresh and evergreen as the love with a funnybone.
— GEORGE JEAN NATHAN

Romantic Resources

#19 *Romantic Homes*
PO Box 344
Mt. Morris, IL 61054-7614

#203 Council on Foundations
Call 202-467-0427

#420 M&Ms
Call 800-627-7852

#507 Rosemary's Procelain Art
RR 1 Box 99A
Milford, NE 68405

#768 Condor Flag Company
Call 800-342-3524

#804 DeBeers
Call 800-FOREVER

#815 Smitten Mittens
Call 888-749-7283

#841 Pelham Hotel
15 Cromwell Place
South Kensington Place
London, England
Call 800-553-6674

#877 Country Living Travel
Call 888-268-9584

#1051 Patricia Dupont
PO Box 211
Rowayton, CT 06853

#1133 Cumberland Falls State Park
Call 606-528-4124

#1146 *Victoria*
PO Box 7150
Red Oak, Iowa 51591

#1312 Cash's of Ireland
Call 800-223-8100